The Essentials of Job Negotiations

The Essentials of Job Negotiations

Proven Strategies for Getting What You Want

Terri R. Kurtzberg and Charles E. Naquin

 PRAEGER

AN IMPRINT OF ABC-CLIO, LLC
Santa Barbara, California • Denver, Colorado • Oxford, England

Library of Congress Cataloging-in-Publication Data

Kurtzberg, Terri R.
  The essentials of job negotiations : proven strategies for getting what you want / Terri R. Kurtzberg and Charles E. Naquin.
      p. cm.
  Includes bibliographical references and index.
  ISBN 978–0–313–39584–0 (pbk. : alk. paper) — ISBN 978–0–313–39585–7 (ebook)
1. Employment interviewing. 2. Job offers. 3. Employee fringe benefits. 4. Wages.
5. Negotiation in business. I. Naquin, Charles E. II. Title.
HF5549.5.I6K87   2011
650.14′4—dc23   2011030902

ISBN: 978–0–313–39584–0
EISBN: 978–0–313–39585–7

15 14 13 12 11   1 2 3 4 5

This book is also available on the World Wide Web as an eBook.
Visit www.abc-clio.com for details.

Praeger
An Imprint of ABC-CLIO, LLC

ABC-CLIO, LLC
130 Cremona Drive, P.O. Box 1911
Santa Barbara, California 93116-1911

This book is printed on acid-free paper ∞

Manufactured in the United States of America

To our students, who inspired us and tirelessly shared their stories with us, and to our families, who gave us the time to make this book a reality.

Contents

INTRODUCTION

Fears and Falsehoods

WHY YOU SHOULD GIVE YOUR BEST TO THIS NEGOTIATION (WHY YOU NEED THIS BOOK)

Congratulations! If you're interested in this book, chances are that you have several things going for you in terms of your future career. You have notable accomplishments under your belt (whether educational, professional, or both) that make you attractive as a potential employee. You are living in an age when traditional job opportunities exist alongside new opportunities generated by changing technologies. However, these opportunities have barriers to entry that can be both exhausting and potentially demoralizing, including the job search, (multiple) interviews, and ultimately, the job negotiation itself.

Your employment package is perhaps one of the most important negotiations you are likely to encounter. It will influence your future income, your personal and professional relationships, and your lifestyle. Perhaps unfairly, in many cases your current salary means more than your performance in predicting the value of your next employment opportunity. This is particularly relevant since most employees find themselves switching companies, sometimes repeatedly, over the course of a career. Yet many who reach the stage of being offered an employment contract, especially those without the benefit of training in negotiations, tend to accept the first offer, pretty much at face value, with little effort (if any at all) toward bettering the package.

Many professionals get through the interview and offer stages with relative ease, only to stumble upon, or completely forego, the job negotiation out of fear and mistaken ideas about what to do and how to do it. They fear making the other side angry by asking for more than what they were offered. They fear appearing greedy. They fear being rejected in their requests. And, they fear the risk of having the offer withdrawn entirely. These fears of doing something wrong are rooted in false assumptions about negotiations, and lead to missed opportunities. Even seasoned professionals can fall victim to myths and biases that impede their success in working out the details of an employment contract. Once we clear up those assumptions, you should be more willing and able to proceed with effective negotiations.

THE BIG MYTHS TO OVERCOME: THE SIX FALSEHOODS

Novices (and even some experienced but poorly trained negotiators) seem to fall victim to several popular but faulty assumptions, or myths, that can result in their failing to negotiate the best possible employment package. Instead of saying "myth," we could just as easily say "falsehood," because they are simply not true. If you find yourself falling victim to any of these myths outlined here, then you should quickly dispel it, recognizing it for what it is—a falsehood. This section offers you a chance to discover the most commonly held misconceptions about job negotiations as well as to be introduced to many of the topics that we will cover in detail throughout the book. Not falling victim to these common false assumptions will allow you to get into an open frame of mind for the insights and tips to follow in the rest of the book.

Falsehood # 1: The job offer is a "standard" package and is "not negotiable." My only choices are to respond either "yes" or "no."

This is a common line we have heard from many employers in many different industries. This is usually false. Whereas a "standard" package may be offered, and the organization may want to keep new hires on a relatively equal footing, most organizations have some flexibility in what they offer to prospective employees. While the standard package notion may hold true for some elements of a negotiation, it is rarely true for all elements. For example, it may be the case that the signing bonus is an area where the employer is particularly resistant to negotiating, since raising the entry-level bonus for one new hire might result in a new precedent being set for other new hires at this level. However, this same employer might be more than willing to consider aiding a graduating student in paying back some school-related expenses such as certification prep courses and exams, or even student loans (we have seen all of these covered). A key insight here is to remain focused on the value of the *total* package, and resist the urge to attend exclusively to the value of an individual issue. Explicitly telling the potential employer that there are student expenses to address opens the door for the employer to help meet these needs and potentially raises the value of the total employment package without compromising the internal company "standards." This example also provides an early glimpse into the benefits of being each (1) proactive, (2) creative, and (3) willing to share information during the negotiation, as we cover more extensively in Chapter 4.

In summary, we hear the rhetoric of this particular myth from many candidates (some may even be assured it is a firm fact by an HR representative), but from our experience, the "nonnegotiable package" is rarely etched in stone and is just part of the dance from the employer's perspective. Instead, it is common for an employer to put forth a package initially and actually expect to make a counteroffer if necessary—in fact, they may have a counteroffer already planned before you even respond. Keep in mind, there is typically a *range* of acceptable entry-level packages within an organization, and this range gets broader as the hierarchical ladder is climbed. Higher-level positions, as well as higher-level candidates, tend to be more unique, and thus there is more inherent flexibility in negotiations for those positions.

Falsehood # 2: I have been working and performing well for a long time, so my outstanding credentials will land me a great job offer/raise/ promotion.

This may be so, but you shouldn't count on it. Employment contracts are influenced by a number of factors other than objective performance or future potential. There are many competing demands for the attention of those in charge of hiring and promotion decisions, and you are sharing the spotlight not only with other candidates in the field, but also with others inside the company. There is also a regrettable tendency to overweigh the importance of whoever has had the most recent big accomplishment or has been brought to mind the most recently (a decision making bias based on selective recall and the recency bias), even if your own credentials should objectively give you the upper hand. And, unfortunately, today's employment landscape seems to be particularly insensitive to internal accomplishments, as compared to that of previous generations.

Gone are the days when it was typical for an employee to work within the same company for his or her entire career, rising steadily through the ranks. While this is by no means impossible today, it is certainly no longer the norm. In fact, a number of our former students have found the fastest track to promotion and better pay is to quit a job to work for a competitor at more pay, only to negotiate being rehired by their original company a few years later, with a promotion and even greater compensation! Unfortunately, relying on internal promotions based solely on evaluations of your performance may not get you to where you want to be. Given this tendency toward a lack of (internal) recognition, it is not a good idea to rely on your objective qualifications alone. Instead, if you are aware of the nuances of job negotiations, you can then be proactive in creating the best possible situation.

Falsehood # 3: If I start negotiating, I will offend or otherwise put off my future employer.

This assumption is simply not true. Not only will the company be prepared for your request to negotiate, but they would like to make you happy if they can. Once they have made you an offer, they have signaled that they actually do want you to join the firm. They may even respect your business acumen all the more if you do initiate such a dialogue and conduct this negotiation in a professional manner. Of course, there are things that you could say that could ruin your chances of being offered the job (for example, asking for double what you think you might actually get "just to see" if it might work out). But any reasonable requests will in all probability be taken seriously by the other side. The worst that can happen is that they will say no, and you can still take the offer as it was if you so decide. In our combined 30 years of dealing with job negotiations, we have never heard of an offer being pulled simply for requesting a chance to revise some of its elements. The key is being wholly respectful at all times to ensure you don't create any ill will with your future employer. In other words, it's not just what you say, but also how you say it. And while it is not necessarily *required* for you to negotiate the offer, when people decide not to negotiate at all, it is generally because they are afraid of the negotiation process. We hope that identifying this falsehood, combined with the skills outlined in this book, will help you to become more comfortable with the ins and outs of the process so that you can conduct your next job negotiation with confidence and skill.

Falsehood # 4: I'm just not good at job negotiations (or perhaps any negotiation, for that matter).

While some people do seem to have personality characteristics that make them more comfortable with negotiations in general, without training, most people are uneasy with this situation. Individuals become good negotiators through training, practice, and receiving feedback on their methods and style. In other words, negotiation is a learned skill, and everyone can improve. Given this, even if you lack confidence now, with a little effort you can improve your skills and, subsequently, your confidence level. Books such as this one, classes or seminars, and practical application are all avenues that you can use to improve your negotiation skills. Remember, if you have done something many times, it generally loses its ability to intimidate you. Getting accustomed to the ins and outs of job negotiation is one way to get more comfortable with the process.

Falsehood # 5: I have negotiated before (maybe even a lot), so I should be fine by just going in and thinking on my feet during the discussion.

One of the secrets that good negotiators know is the importance of effectively preparing for an upcoming negotiation. There is a tremendous amount of information to process, critical decisions to be made, and strategic thinking that go into planning for a successful negotiation in any context, and the job negotiation is no exception. Planning, researching, deciding about contingencies, forming questions, benchmarking, etc., will all help to lead the actual negotiation to a successful conclusion. Chapter 1 will walk you through the steps to take in order to master the planning process. Wait-and-see approaches can lead instead to panic and less-than-ideal, rushed decisions.

Unfortunately, experience alone will not necessarily get you the skills you need for several reasons. First, after a negotiation is concluded, you do not typically get to know whether you could have negotiated a better deal. Instead, it is more common for the other side to appear "squeezed" even if there was significantly more you could have gained simply by asking for it. Next, people tend to put a positive spin on their actions and see their behavior as effective, whether or not they actually acted in the best way (known as the positive illusion bias). Similarly, even when they do recognize their own failures, they have a very strong instinct to explain them away as due to some sort of external constraint (the other person was unreasonable, the market was terrible, etc.) in ways that release them from any responsibility. On the other hand, when they succeed, they are more than happy to recognize their own role in the action. This is problematic in particular when trying to learn from real-time experience, because people don't always recognize what they need to be doing differently. People also tend to have some misleading instincts about the need to take big risks to win big in negotiations—and the need to trust their instincts and "think on their feet" during negotiations instead of systematically and effectively planning their own course of action. While risky strategies may sometimes be wise, and indeed you will need to react in real time to some parts of the negotiation process, the well-planned negotiation is by far the most successful one. Thus, taking time to study and learn about negotiations before the actual moment arrives is the key to becoming more effective in this, as in other, negotiation settings.

Falsehood # 6: Within my culture, negotiating an employment offer is not an acceptable practice.

This may have been true at one time, but it is growing increasingly false, as the world becomes more and more of a global community—and thus, we list it as a myth. At one time, it was the norm to not negotiate the employment contract even here within the United States, where doing so is now commonplace. The same is happening around the world in the for-profit sectors. Indeed, in today's global economy, business practices are becoming standardized in many regards. For contemporary employees, that means the employment contract is becoming more and more negotiable, no matter where you are located geographically. Among cross-cultural scholars, in fact, there is a growing perspective that business is becoming its own transnational culture, often referred to as the "third culture" after national and organizational cultures. We have had students successfully negotiate their employment terms in all major regions of the world, including North and South America, Asia, Europe, the Middle East, Africa, and Australia. This is not to say that modifying one's approach to negotiating as a function of culture is not warranted. As we describe in Chapter 8, there are clear advantages to taking different approaches for different cultures, and one should alter the negotiation strategy as appropriate, but the job negotiation itself should still occur.

Unfortunately, falling victim to any one of these myths is almost guaranteed to lead to a suboptimal employment package. These falsehoods are impediments to your career. Put them out of your mind. Instead of having these barriers stand in your way, place your focus on acquiring the necessary skills for negotiating a job contract well, and becoming familiar with all the nuances that the process entails. When reading this book, remember to check your "fears and falsehoods" at the door, and open your mind to a more productive and scientifically proven way of thinking about job negotiations.

OVERVIEW OF THE BOOK

As negotiation professors and scholars, we want your job negotiation to serve to better your career and life. To meet this specific objective, we have compiled all of our experiences into a single book and culled key lessons from over 50 years of high-quality research in negotiations, psychology, decision making, and communications. We have applied this cumulative body of knowledge to the contemporary marketplace, yielding a source of cutting-edge negotiation strategies as they apply to the job negotiation context. The book is peppered with true accounts from both business school students and other working professionals (accountants, lawyers, consultants, engineers, etc.) who have walked this road before you. (Of course, all names and identifying features have been changed to protect the privacy of those who contributed their stories.)

This book is for you if you are (or want to be) engaged in negotiations to improve your employment terms. This can range from an internal transfer within an organization, a raise and/or a promotion to a new position, or an entirely new relationship with a company or organization. We make no differentiation between internal and external moves or between lateral, upward, and downward movements on the hierarchical ladder. The bottom line is that if you are a business professional changing your employment contract in any way, you will benefit from the knowledge and strategies within this book.

In the rest of this book we will make sure you are prepared for each and every aspect of the job negotiation process. After the lessons on preparing yourself and what to expect from the other side, Chapter 1 also covers information on emotions at the table, and how to remain calm in the face of an intimidating situation. In Chapter 2, we walk you through the best ways to make a good impression from the moment you step into the first interview in order to create the excitement needed for both sides to commit to a successful negotiation. Chapter 3 covers the importance of delaying the conversation about salary until the appropriate moment in the negotiations. Chapter 4 dives into the details about how to work with different aspects of the deal to create trade-offs that feel fair to both sides and offer value for your bottom line. Chapter 5 covers research on communication and persuasion, and offers lessons on how to get your points heard the most effectively. Chapter 6 reviews the effects of negotiating via e-mail, and allows you to recognize and overcome some of the common pitfalls of that process. Chapter 7 tackles the issue of using headhunters or other agents as go-betweens in your negotiations, and gives you a chance to think through how to manage that relationship to your advantage. Chapter 8 looks at special circumstances such as family businesses, poor economic climates, and cross-cultural negotiations and analyzes the ways in which these contexts can change your needs and theirs. Lastly, Chapter 9 moves into negotiating your relationship with your new employer as you start your job. Chapter 10 provides a summary of the most common traps in the job negotiation process, and tips for avoiding each. Overall, the chapters in this book offer insights, strategies, and examples to help guide your employment terms toward the best possible deal. We hope that by the end of the book, you will not only stop being afraid of the negotiation, but will actively look forward to the process since you will have the skills and insights to be a success at the job negotiation game.

ONE

Behind-the-Scenes Preparation: Before You Even Walk in the Door

As with any negotiation, effective preparation is critical to success, yet this is the area in which people most consistently fall short. As negotiations professors, we can always spot those who failed to prepare adequately for their job negotiations because, at the conclusion, they cannot explain why a deal was either appealing or unappealing to them other than "it just felt right" (or not). This logic signals that the candidate most likely stumbled through the details of the negotiation without taking full advantage of the opportunity. Proper preparation will never work to your disadvantage in a job negotiation, but it can help you tremendously.

Don't be discouraged by the idea that you will never get perfect information about what the employer wants or may be willing to offer. In particular, information about what your potential employers are able and willing to offer (based on their budgets and other limitations), what their special interests may be, and where their bottom line is can be difficult to come by. Having such complete information would make the job negotiation very simple, but it isn't realistic. Instead, negotiations inherently contain uncertainty. Although you may be able to estimate lots of information about your potential employers, you can never predict with total certainty what they will say or do. Nonetheless, information is a source of power in a negotiation, and you would be well advised to do as much research as you can about them and as much planning as you can about your own needs and wants. These steps will help you to make and justify your requests more persuasively.

In this chapter, we outline the steps to take in preparing for the job negotiation, which includes knowing your own preferences as well as understanding the company's perspective. We discuss the difference between acting and reacting in negotiations, and being clear with yourself about the difference between what you *need* out of a job and what you would ideally *want* but could live without if necessary. Finally, we cover some common questions encountered in the preparation stage.

"GUT-FEEL" REACTIONS VERSUS PROACTIVE PLANNING

Most novices in the area of negotiations feel that successful negotiations hinge primarily on being able to think on their feet during the negotiation, and to react appropriately to whatever is thrown at them from the other side. We like to call those using this type of approach the "gut-feel" negotiators, or those who rely on logic such as "I will know it's the right thing to do because it will feel right" at the expense of systematic planning and decision making. While there are certainly moments when you need to react in real time, taking the "gut-feel" approach as your strategy often results in grave missed opportunities. You lose out on the opportunity not just to react in the negotiation, but to act—and to act in a persuasive, reasonable, and logical manner that can help you reach your goals.

Research shows that when there is a sense of unequal power between the two parties in a negotiation (and most job candidates tend to feel that the recruiter is the more powerful party), it is the player with *lower* power who is responsible for driving solutions of higher gain.[1] In other words, though most of the time candidates prefer to wait and let the recruiter control the discussion in job negotiations, this approach results in a lost opportunity to get your own ideas and suggestions onto the table. The message here is clear. *You* need to put yourself in the driver's seat to make positive things happen in a job negotiation. This is often not an easy task when you have another person to contend with, and one who may appear intimidating to boot. To do this, you need effective plans at your fingertips and not just your "gut feel" or intuition, however finely it may be tuned.

TIP

Preparation is the key to being a proactive negotiator instead of being someone who flies by the seat of the pants and is only able to react.

In fact, the amount of planning that you do ahead of time is the single best predictor of the level of success you will achieve in your deal.

Properly preparing for negotiations essentially boils down to reducing uncertainty by having a better understanding of the needs of both sides. Table 1.1 gives you a template for making sure you have been thorough

Table 1.1.   Planning Table: The Seven Key Insights for Effective Planning

1a. What do you *need* out of this offer (i.e., what are the deal-breakers for you?) 1. 2. 3. 4. 5.	1b. What do you think the company *need* out of a candidate? 1. 2. 3. 4. 5.
2a. What do you *want* out of this offer (i.e., what does your target/ ideal job look like)? 1. 2. 3. 4. 5.	2b. What do you think the company *want* out of a candidate? 1. 2. 3. 4. 5.

3. What would a really great offer look like for you, roughly? (A realistic stretch, not a "pie in the sky.")

4. What would a minimally acceptable offer look like for you, roughly?

5. What information should you make sure you share with the other side to explain to them how you will meet their *needs* well and even fulfill some of their *wants*?

6a. What options do you have besides this job?	6b. What options do you think the company has besides hiring you?

7. Based on the above, how powerful do you think you are relative to the other side (i.e., how badly do you think they need you, and how badly do you want this job)?

in preparing for the upcoming negotiation. Now that you have had a glimpse at the whole table, we will explain its elements in greater detail one at a time (see Appendix A for a blank copy of this table to use).

Part 1: You

The first aspect of planning is getting to know your own needs and wishes. Although this may seem intuitively obvious, we are always surprised to realize that very few people actually spend the time to do this thoroughly. This stage is essentially an exercise in self-examination. What do you need, as a minimum, out of your job? What elements do you want, but could live without? How do you figure out which elements in the contract you are willing to sacrifice in order to attain others? As a first step, separating out the list of your *wants* from the list of your *needs* is a valuable exercise (Steps 1a and 2a in the Planning Table). *Wants* are the things you would ideally like to see in the package but might be willing to forego in order to get the job. In contrast, *needs* are deal-breakers that you simply could not proceed without.

We have engaged in this activity with hundreds of people, and an interesting pattern has emerged. When asked to generate a list of their requirements (or their *needs* for a job), most people list things like good pay, a decent vacation and benefits package, at least reasonably interesting work, and the potential for career growth opportunities (of course, your real list needs to be much more precise in terms of actual numbers and goals). When asked what they would ideally want out of a deal but not necessarily need to have for a deal, the *wants* list that emerges is remarkably similar to the *needs* list, but with greater quantities for each item: not just good but *great* salary, not just some but *more* vacation time, *very* interesting work, and *assured* career growth.

The decision of what and how much of something belongs in the *want* column versus the *need* column is entirely an individual one, and the line between them can be subtle. No two lists are going to be identical, so it really is up to you to spend the time and do the hard work of considering what is critically important versus what is desirable but optional in the final decision of what you are willing to accept. For those just beginning their professional careers, it can be difficult work to pinpoint the exact line between requirement and desire. For experienced professionals, it becomes easier to delineate the two. No matter what your level of experience, however, it is a worthwhile endeavor to truly understand where you should dig your heels in during the negotiation (to get your *needs*) and where you should still aim for your *wants* but not risk the entire deal over the issue at hand. You will find a list of potentially negotiable items in Appendix B to help get you started.

Though it may feel like you already know exactly what you *want* or *need* out of a job, we have seen very intelligent and motivated people fail to quantify their preferences in this way and suffer because of it. The real-life situations described here show how a lack of clarity in these areas can lead to poor decisions.

TWO TRUE STORIES

Mike and his wife Kelly were both professionals on the job market. When Mike was offered a job in another city, he took it, only to quit soon afterward as it proved difficult for Kelly to also relocate to the area, and untenable for them to live in two different locations.

In another situation, Amanda turned down a job with a base salary of $110K because she was hoping to get one for over $120K instead. When that didn't materialize, she ended up taking one for only $105K.

In the first example, Mike confused a *need* (the need to have job opportunities for both spouses in the same location) with a *want* (it would have been nicer to have this, but it was not required for him to say yes). He and Kelly were not honest with themselves about their *need* to be colocated. We see the opposite mistake happening in the second example, in which Amanda thought the base salary of $120K (or more) was a *need*, when in truth it later proved itself to be a *want*. She would rather have more, but she was obviously willing to take a job for less. Knowing more precisely how these issues actually ranked on their *wants*-versus-*needs* scales might have saved each of them from making a costly mistake.

TIP

Keep in mind that *needs* and *wants* are distinct, and don't confuse them in a negotiation. If you receive an offer above your *needs*, you should carefully consider it before declining. On the other side, do not walk away from an offer simply because it did not meet your *wants* (unless you are sure that there are better offers available).

Once you have your list of *needs* and *wants*, you can start to assemble the items into possible employment packages to give yourself a sense of what an offer should look like for your particular case. While we cover this topic in much greater detail later in the book (see Chapter 4), even at this early stage, you should start to have some sense of what your ideal package looks like, while still being realistic about what's reasonable (Step 3 in the Planning Table). Then determine what your bare-minimum package looks like (Step 4). Note also that sometimes one wish comes at the expense of another. For example, many people struggle with the trade-off between how much money they want and how much time away from the office they want. Sure, all of us would prefer to have large amounts of money, time off, flexibility, interesting work, and prospects for advancement, but deciding ahead of time what levels of these (and other) variables you *need* as opposed to *want* can help guide you when you are in a position to discuss possible trade-offs (more on this idea to come in Chapter 4).

Lastly, though this might feel less intuitive, it is important to redo this whole exercise of identifying your *needs* and *wants* for yourself for *each* new position you are considering. Variables such as location, job title, industry, or company reputation can greatly influence how important the other factors become. For example, let's assume you have two competing job offers from firms in different parts of the country—one is in New York City and one is in Oklahoma City, and both are offering you about $90,000. Clearly, those are not equivalent offers even though they offer objectively identical salaries. Your *wants* and *needs* lists don't survive in isolation, but instead need to be thought of together as parts of packages. How they differ might depend on the person. One might say, "Of course these numbers are different! For $90,000 I can live like a king in Oklahoma City while I can barely make ends meet in New York City," while another might say, "Of course they are not equal! You couldn't pay me enough to move to Oklahoma City when I could be right in the center of things in New York City."

The bottom line is that only you can decide what's important, and how important it is for you. Our advice is to do the hard work of explicitly (in other words, write it all down) exploring your preferences on potential issues ahead of time, before the actual job negotiation begins. Your employment package is too important to take the impulsive fly-by-the-seat-of-your-pants, gut-feel approach. Instead, take the time to prepare properly and be a proactive negotiator by knowing your own *wants* and *needs*. This easy task significantly tilts the odds in favor of your making a good decision.

TIP

Know yourself well. For each different job opportunity that arises, be thorough in knowing what would be minimally acceptable (your *needs*) and what it will really take to make you absolutely delighted with the offer (your *wants*).

Part 2: The Other Side—Your Future Employer

While it is important to understand your own *wants* and *needs*, understanding the company's perspective and gathering information on *their wants* and *needs* are potentially even more critical. Whether you are buying or selling, negotiating a contract of any kind, or engaging in any other type of negotiated settlement, take the time to put yourself in the other side's shoes. Even if you don't ever get perfect information, any insights into how the other side sees things, what their interests and needs are, as well as their limits and other options, is the equivalent of negotiation gold.

Thus, your next step in the preparation task (Steps 1b and 2b on the Planning Table) is to create another *wants*-versus-*needs* list, this time from the firm's perspective (instead of about yourself). What do you imagine they *need* out of a job candidate? What might they *want* beyond that? What is it that you can tell them to make a convincing case that you are able not just to meet their *needs*, but also to satisfy some of their *wants* (Step 5 in the Planning Table)? Remember, your primary task as a candidate is to "sell" yourself to the firm as someone who will more than meet their needs. The job search is an announcement by the firm to the world that they have an unmet set of needs—you should convince them that you are the one who will deliver value in exactly the areas that they require and more. Having given hard thought to both your side and their side of the negotiation, you are now in a much better position to strategically sell yourself to get your own needs met while demonstrating that you are the right one to take care of their needs as well.

Next comes an analysis of the power that you and the company each bring to the table. Does the recruiting firm with the job to offer and the final say on who will get the position always have more power? Or can it be the candidate who has the particular skill set that the company needs who is in the more powerful position? In truth, it could be either, and there are usually two predictors—level of experience and number of alternative job offers. Entry-level professionals tend to have less power than experienced ones, but power also depends on the number of attractive options each side has *other than* the deal being considered at this time. This makes intuitive sense, since a firm with dozens of equally qualified candidates for a single position has the power of choice and thus the luxury of not needing any one particular candidate all that much. Meanwhile, an applicant with a unique skill set who is sitting on a stack of offers from firms who have been unsuccessfully trying to find just such a person can also be in a position of power. A firm who has had trouble keeping individuals in a particular job may also be desperate to give it some stability.

How do you find out about these relative levels of power if the information is not forthcoming? You already know your own situation, and should put it in Step 6a of the Planning Table. You can then try to gather some information from the other side by asking questions such as, "How long has the position been open?" "How long was the last employee in this role?" and the like, to fill in Step 6b on the table. Then, you will be equipped to move on to Step 7, where you compare the two lists and get an assessment of where you stand going into the negotiations. It is just as helpful to know you have little power in a job negotiation as it is to realize you have the power advantage.

TIP

Spend time thinking about and researching the company's perspective, possible needs, and their other options for this open position. Compare them with your own to understand your power relative to theirs.

SIDEBAR: OFFERS AS POWER

A job offer in itself is a source of power, since it provides you with an opportunity for employment as well as serves to signal your worth to other potential employers. Thus, from a purely rational economic-maximization perspective, to get more power in the employment marketplace means to collect offers (as many as possible) and keep them valid (for as long as possible). The employing companies, on the other hand, have a different agenda. Ideally, they want to fill their open position with the best available candidate as quickly as possible while expending minimal resources. In reality, because of these misaligned interests, the timing of job opportunities does not always work to your advantage, as companies are resistant to letting you hold onto offers for long periods of time just so you can compare it to other options. In fact, they often get anxious at the mere suggestion that you are still considering other jobs.

But as much as we would like to consider all our job opportunities simultaneously, we rarely get that kind of perfect information in any area of life. You don't get to see all the possible houses you might want to buy at once. Instead, you have to decide on each one in sequence, understanding that if you do not bid on it, it may not be available at a later time. Similarly, you do not get to meet all of the people you might want to marry at once and then choose the best among the options. We meet people continuously throughout our lives and make decisions as we go about whether each is someone we want to spend time with. Job opportunities are the same. You may be lucky enough to consider a few options simultaneously, but more often than not, each opportunity appears in a one-at-a-time format. Knowing that it is an imperfect process ahead of time will hopefully help get you through the frustrations that you may encounter.

It may even be for the best that you probably won't have 10, or even 5, offers to consider at the same time. In a study of job seekers, people who took the first good opportunity ended up *happier* with their choice in the long run than did those who kept searching until they found the best position.[2] Why? Because if and when something turns out to be less than ideal in the new job, those who searched long and hard and considered multiple options blamed themselves more for an imperfect decision. Take comfort in the idea that a few offers, and a good-enough fit, might be the best thing that could happen.

WHAT DOES THE COMPANY WANT, GENERALLY SPEAKING?

This section provides a list of some of the basic motivations and perspectives that most employers have. However, this discussion obviously cannot replace detailed research for any one job, in which you aim to become well versed in what you should expect from a specific company (more on how to do this later in this chapter) as well as the norms for the industry as a whole. Instead, understanding these concepts may allow you to better appreciate the employer's interests and actions. You yourself may even have been on the other side of the hiring table, or perhaps what happens from the perspective of the employer is shrouded in some level of mystery (or misunderstanding) for you. Even if these points are not new to you, it is worth bringing them back to the forefront of your thinking before you jump into your next job negotiation.

Employers want the best person they can get for the job. This is pretty self-explanatory. But this also means that they do not typically hire someone they think is only okay. Instead, they will tend to wait for someone they think is truly great and whom they are sure they will love. From your perspective, then, getting a job offer is a process of getting someone in the company to be inspired about you.

Clarification: Employers want the best person they can get for the job who isn't an ass. When the market is such that there are a lot of people who are qualified for a job, the one that tends to be offered the position is the one that employers most like being around—the one they would not mind working late with, or going out to lunch and dinner with. This is sometimes called the "no asshole rule."[3]

Employers have constraints. Employers may appear irrational when in reality, they are simply constrained. Imagine that you have two job offers, and the company you want to work for has a lower salary offer. You ask the company you want to work for if they can match the higher competing salary, and they reply that they cannot, fully realizing they may lose you to the competing company. Although it could be the case that they don't want you, or they want you but not badly enough to increase your salary, in our experience, it is an unlikely possibility. It is more likely that when a company does not match a competing offer, it is because of an internal constraint of some kind about which you may not be aware. For example, internal equity, or the idea that they cannot (or rather, are not willing to) pay you more than others at the same level who already work at that company, is a driving concern for many businesses. Constraints such as this are part of organizational life, and you should recognize that getting resistance to your requests may well be for rational reasons other than their lack of desire to hire you. In the words of one frustrated HR representative, "I know most people don't believe this, but we really are not trying to screw you over. We actually do try to put our best offer on the table. Before I worked in this job I thought there was much more wiggle room than there actually is—sure, we can sometimes come up a little if we feel like you're being honest with us and giving us a good reason why you're asking, but it's less than you'd think. We *do* want to hire you once our line managers decide on you, but we're constrained."

Employers hire for the long haul. Most HR departments are keenly aware of how much they spend searching for new talent, and then training their new hires. They are aware, as well, that these costs and investments are not recoverable if they should lose you shortly after you start. As a result, to protect the organization's future interests, companies would like you to not only take the job, but also to be happy and satisfied with the job (and your compensation package) so that you want to stay there for the long term. Otherwise, they run the risk of losing an employee in whom they have invested significant amounts of time and money only to redo the process with somebody else.

Employers expect to negotiate. The hiring process is full of pomp and ceremony: the interview, invitations to dinners and parties, meeting the boss, getting the offer, getting a formal contract, and finally, negotiating the employment terms. Again, even though many HR departments may resist, they are prepared to hear you out if you make a reasonable request to negotiate. Indeed, they expect the negotiation, as most professional managers will explore altering some terms of their contract. From an employer's perspective, they don't mind negotiating job contracts as long as the requests are reasonable, can be justified, and are presented in a respectful manner.

While employers don't mind negotiating, they also want a quick end to the process. Nobody likes spending too much time on the job negotiation process. If it is not going to work out with you, they want to quickly find somebody else to fill the needed role. If you have done your research, know the industry norms, and are explicit about what you want in your counteroffer and why you want it (topics we cover later in the book), the negotiation process should progress at a reasonable pace for both sides. If you properly prepare for the job negotiation, then, you should be able to reach a deal you both are satisfied with, or to decide to walk away, through the course of a few exchanges.

Employers do not want to renegotiate after a deal is made. Most employers do not like to play games. Job negotiations are serious undertakings, and once agreed upon, they are considered done. The negotiation is over. The focus now turns back to the work.

Employers want a reasonable answer to the question of why you are leaving (or have left) your previous place of employment. This comes up again and again when we talk to hiring managers. Unfortunately, there are so many wrong answers here. If you answer that it is because your last boss was impossible to work for, a red flag goes up warning of the possibility that it is you yourself who does not know how to work well with others. If you state that the previous company was always in a state of flux with changing goals and priorities, another red flag goes up warning that you might not be able to keep up with today's fast-paced market. In fact, the consensus on the best answer seems to be to talk about yourself and not the previous company at all, with statements like "I wanted the chance to develop different skills" or "I was ready for a new challenge." Generic? Yes. Boring? Perhaps. But not likely to alienate someone who doesn't yet know you by showing yourself to be a complainer of any kind.

Employers are motivated to find information about you from sources other than those you yourself provide. In this day and age, you should assume that little information is private. In addition to formal background checks, many employers will do some informal searching about your background, which can mean anything from calling a colleague of theirs at your last place of employment to using search engines and social networking websites to see if anything unprofessional turns up. More than one person has lost a job because of questionable pictures posted on the Internet, even decades after their original posting. Whether this practice is right or wrong, it is now commonplace, and you should search for your own name online and clean up whatever content you would not want your prospective boss to see. Don't underestimate how much access a motivated person can have to information about your life.

TIP

Think about whether you, as a hiring manager, would want to hire you, as a candidate.

PREPARING YOURSELF: EMOTIONS AT THE TABLE

Most of the time, negotiating makes people nervous. Some people negotiate practically daily at their jobs and thus get accustomed to the process. But negotiating for yourself and your livelihood can make even the strongest negotiator feel a little weak in the knees. We would like to introduce a little bit of the research on how emotions play a role in negotiations so that you can help yourself separate out the nerves from the logic and stay focused on the deal you want and need to achieve.

We start at the end: how do people react to the final negotiated deal? Unfortunately, all too often, the answer is irrationally. Most people approach negotiations from what's called a fixed-pie mind-set, which translates into feeling that if the other side seems too happy with the deal, it automatically means you must have been "taken" and thus should be less happy with your own outcome.[4] In other words, people with *identical* outcomes in a simulated negotiation suddenly felt worse about their own negotiated deal if they were told only one bit of extra information, which was that the other side is happy with the deal that was made. That's not necessarily logical, since it could well be that the other side was able to achieve their goals (hiring a great candidate for a package that was within the allotted budget and in the location where there was the most need) *and* you were able to achieve your goals (getting a great job with good pay in a stable company, with good colleagues, a clear path to career growth, and the desired chance to relocate). Neither you nor the employer took from each other on issues important to each. In other words, job negotiations are not a "fixed pie" where one side's gain automatically comes at the expense of the other.

In regard to being satisfied with the deal, people seem to care more about their subjective valuation of the deal in question (in large part cued by whether or not they felt there was more value they *could* have gotten out of the deal), as opposed to the objective economic outcomes that they actually achieved. These subjective valuations of their compensation actually seem to be better predictors of future job satisfaction and turnover than are the actual objective salary numbers![5] In short, this means that people are much happier with their own deal (and even their subsequent job) if the other side has said, or implied, that the package contains the highest amounts that could have been offered. This has been explained in part by the "face-threat" instinct that people have. A face-threat is the feeling that someone else has gotten the best of you (or even insulted you with demeaning offers or ultimatums). This feeling makes people very uncomfortable even if they have in fact received what they set out to get from the situation.[6]

Even knowledge of a negotiator's reputation can influence how you negotiate and cause you to perceive the behaviors of the other as more negative or positive than you might have otherwise.[7] For example, knowing that the other side is considered to be a tough negotiator might make you more certain that each offer is designed to squeeze you, whether or not that's actually the case. Particularly if you feel you are in the lower-power position in the negotiation, you are more likely to assume that the other side is trying to take advantage of you. This may even make you misread cooperative signals as competitive ones and preemptively hold back on issues you might have otherwise been willing to offer or concede.[8]

TIP

Don't be fooled by the "game" of negotiation: keep your eyes on the end-state goal and try not to be too reactive to what you think the other side is up to.

The next important thing to know about how emotions influence negotiations is that those who feel in a lower-status position (as most job candidates do) are overly susceptible to being influenced by the other side's
emotions. Dealing with a recruiter who appears even slightly hostile or
angry, for example, can make candidates lose focus and yield more value
than they might if they were not exposed to these troubling emotional
tones from the other side.[9] On the flip side, positive emotions coming
from the more powerful party can influence trust and the quality of the
final deal for both sides, whereas positive emotions from the lower-
power negotiator do not have the same effects.[10] This does not imply that
you should diminish your positive manner in your negotiations. Instead,
we know that positive negotiators are the ones with whom others are most
likely to close a deal, and with whom they prefer to plan future business
interactions.[11] Clearly, getting the deal done as well as paving the way
for a positive working relationship are among the goals of any job negotiation, so remaining positive is advisable.

PREPARATION FAQ

To Whom Should I Be Talking in Order to Get the Inside Scoop on a Company?

There is a lot of information you would want to know from someone on
the inside of a particular company. The best person to talk to is someone
who is doing the job that you want at the firm you are interested in, or perhaps a close peer to the position. Are there alumni from your university
who might be working at the company you are dealing with, for example?
You should be in touch with the career center at your university (whether
current, or your alma mater) to find out about making these kinds of contacts. Or, are there others you may know through your personal and professional networks that work in the targeted firm, or even elsewhere in
the same industry? People you know who have recently engaged in a
related-area job search may also be useful sources, having just gathered
this type of information for themselves. (Unfortunately, at least at this
point in time, electronic social networking has failed to live up to much
of its hype, and few people we have worked with have made important
contacts or gathered meaningful information in this way.) Professional
associations may help in some cases, but nothing beats colleagues,
friends, friends of friends, or alumni in their likelihood to willingly share
good information with you. Now is one of the best times to tap into your
network.

> **TIP**
>
> Use your network where possible to get the inside scoop on a company: Alumni, work associates, friends, friends of friends, family, etc.

In addition, finding the right person to question may even be tactfully done as part of your interview process. If you are not scheduled to meet with some of your potential peers in the new workplace, you might ask whether you could have an informal chat with a few people, or even a lunch, to get to know them and the workplace culture a little better.

What Specific Questions Should I Ask Someone Inside the Firm? (The Big Three)

1. What Salary *Range* Should I Expect?

For whatever reason, sharing one's current salary seems to make people nervous. In Western culture, this is considered highly personal information, even though it is to the benefit of almost everyone to have this information be public (only the person at the very top of the pay scale stands to gain little from sharing this information). Asking people direct questions about what they earn is likely to alienate potentially useful sources of information. Instead, people seem to be much more comfortable talking about salary *ranges*. For example, when speaking to a peer in the company you are interviewing with (or someone in the same industry but with a different firm), asking what salary range you might expect to hear is likely to be a better way to broach the topic. In fact, sometimes this question will even yield more and better information, as people may share insights like "most people with this job description seem to make between $80,000 and $95,000, but I do know of one [individual, firm, etc.] for whom it's more like $100,000, but that's because of [more experience, competing offer, better degree, higher cost of living, location, etc.]." Then, of course, you should compare the information you receive with online sources for that profession (see Appendix C for possible sources). Inside information on salary and benefits is tremendously valuable in the job negotiation.

2. What Do You Wish You Had Negotiated Up Front?

Firms are quirky about offers, benefits, and resources. Some resources are standard-issue at one place but can be open to negotiation at another. The only reliable way to learn about these kinds of issues is to talk to someone who is already working for the firm. Perhaps it is wise to make sure that you get a commitment in writing to have your technology upgraded every year, or perhaps that happens automatically. Perhaps you wish to consider some work-from-home time, and find out that these arrangements either happen from the get-go or not at all, or perhaps the firm likes to see people prove themselves for a year or more and then grants these requests once they are happy with your work. There are other examples of opportunities that people may overlook. If you are starting your new job in the middle of the fiscal year, would you remember to ask to be included in that year's bonus payout? Even after asking, it might or might not be possible, but why not find out if it could go your way? What about administrative support? Might you want a budget for conference travel or continuing education classes periodically, and days to accomplish these activities? These are examples of the kinds of issues that don't necessarily get addressed unless *you* raise them. (See Appendix B for a more complete list.) You should also remember that while money is generally the most constrained resource, titles and job descriptions can occasionally have more room for movement, especially in smaller firms. Details like these can make a big difference in your work and life, and being in the know about what to ask for is incredibly helpful.

3. What Was the Tone of Your Job Negotiation Here?

It is also useful to learn from others' experiences how the negotiations themselves tend to proceed, and what the "style" is of the person who is likely to be in charge of negotiating your package.

A TRUE STORY

When Noah was talking to people in his would-be new firm, he received a pretty consistent picture of the head of the group (who served as the recruiter in this case) as a bit of a bulldog on the outside, but one whose bark was worse than his bite. For example, several current workers told him that the recruiter had tried to hurry their decisions by saying things like "I could offer that to you if you say yes right now," but that he had backed down when necessary. Armed with that knowledge, when the same line was used on him, Noah very respectfully told the recruiter, "I'm very interested in this job, but I'm not willing to say yes right this minute. I'm going to need a week to think about it no matter what the offer contains." This was granted to him. He was grateful for the information so that he was able to sidestep the scare tactic instead of either feeling pressured needlessly or doubting the character of the recruiter (and the firm).

TIP

Talk to someone inside the firm, and ask for information about what you should expect in terms of The Big Three: (1) salary range, (2) special details to address, and (3) negotiating style.

What about Websites?

Part of your preparation should include gathering accurate information about the company you are dealing with and how desirable it is to work for that firm. But don't forget that information posted on websites, while readily available and often plentiful, may not be the most accurate in all cases. Unfortunately, we can be overly influenced by whatever we have heard or seen, even if it is inaccurate. This is one of the reasons why advertising is so effective. When considering a company's reputation, therefore, it is critically important to separate out objective information from whatever you may hear or see, positive or negative, from someone with a vested interest in presenting information in a certain light. Websites can be particularly misleading in this way. As a rule, those websites that anonymously post employee comments and perceptions tend to draw out more responses from the dissatisfied employees than from the satisfied ones. On the other hand, those sponsored by the company itself have obviously been crafted to give only positive views. While most people do sense that reading comments from one or two complainers should not influence your impression about a place, we tend to underestimate the degree to which information like this can unconsciously sway our general impressions. Gathering as many data points as you can is truly the best cure for this problem.

What Should I Be Prepared to Ask For?

Many successful job negotiations boil down to the candidate being the one to remember to ask for certain perks. The quick rule of thumb is that the bigger the company (and the lower the level of the position in question), the fewer details that tend to be negotiable. Larger companies *tend* to offer packages that are more standardized, and the issue of precedent tends to be larger for them than for a smaller company that has the ability to tailor offers and packages for each individual person. However, as described earlier, whereas one large company may refuse to negotiate about vacation time and instead offers the same package to everyone, another may be willing to add extra days to sweeten a deal. That said, it is truly impossible to know what is and what is not negotiable until you ask. Some experienced negotiators argue that negotiations have not truly begun until you have heard the word "no."

To illustrate this point for our students, we use an activity called the "Collecting No" exercise.[12] The task is to design requests to ask different people to try to elicit a "no" as the answer. The goal is to keep asking different questions to different people until you receive 10 rejections. Requests can be for anything, but must be legal and possible (i.e., you could not ask someone to fly to the moon), but other than that, anything goes. People typically feel that this will be exceedingly easy, and are later surprised to find that it takes generally between 15 and 20 requests for the collection of 10 "no" responses. Why is this? It turns out that people generally prefer to say yes to each other, to accommodate a request or at least part of the request, rather than offer an outright rejection. Even when the other side needs to refuse, oftentimes the response comes couched as a counteroffer, such as "Well, I can't give you my car but I could lend it to you for a weekend" or "Maybe I can drive you to the train station instead" or some other way to try to meet the interests of your requests. Over the years, students have been shocked to find out that their colleagues, family, friends, and even, in some cases, complete strangers were willing to go to such great lengths as to lend them large sums of money, give or lend them their possessions, and donate their time and energy to helping them out. While these are for the most part different situations from a job negotiation with someone whom you do not yet know, the underlying principle remains the same: you simply don't know for sure what will get a no, a yes, or a maybe until you ask. As an insightful person once put it, "You get half of what you ask for and none of what you don't."

TIP

Don't be the one who simply doesn't ask. You certainly won't get what you have not bothered to request.

SUMMARY

The best-prepared candidates are the ones who (1) know what they *need* and *want*, (2) understand well what to expect from *this* company's negotiations, (3) have thought through how to include as many items of value as possible, and (4) can remain rational, respectful, and positive even in the face of an emotionally charged setting such as a job negotiation. You can help yourself do this through effectively preparing. Planning is not always exciting work, but the benefits will become apparent as soon as you begin the actual negotiation. While it is more intuitive to plan for yourself, also take the time to write down any information you can surmise about the other side's power, motives, alternatives, goals, and bottom line. Finally, don't forget that while offers are a source power, waiting for the perfect offer can make you lose out on an opportunity that could make you happy.

NOTES

1. Mannix, E. A., and M. A. Neale, Power imbalance and the pattern of exchange in dyadic negotiations. *Group Decision and Negotiation*, 2, 1993: 119–133.

2. Schwartz, B., Doing better but feeling worse: Looking for the "best" job undermines satisfaction. *Psychological Science*, 17, 2006: 143–150.

3. Sutton, R., *The no asshole rule: Building a civilized workplace and surviving one that isn't*. New York: Warner Business Books, 2007.

4. Thompson, L., K. L. Valley, and R. M. Kramer, The bittersweet feeling of success: An examination of social perception in negotiation. *Journal of Experimental Social Psychology*, 31, 1995: 467–492.

5. Curhan, J. R., H. A. Elfbein, and G. J. Kildruff, Getting off on the right foot: Subjective value versus economic value in predicting longitudinal job outcomes from job offer negotiations. *Journal of Applied Psychology*, 94, 2009: 524–534.

6. White, J. B., et al., Face threat sensitivity in negotiation: Roadblock to agreement and joint gain. *Organizational Behavior and Human Decision Processes*, 94, 2004: 102–124.

7. Tinsley, C. H., K. M. O'Connor, and B. A. Sullivan, Tough guys finish last: The perils of a distributive reputation. *Organizational Behavior and Human Decision Processes*, 88, 2002: 621–642.

8. Johnson, N. A., and R. B. Cooper, Power and concessions in computer mediated negotiation: An examination of first offers. *MIS Quarterly*, 33, 2009: 147–170.

9. Overbeck, J. R., M. A. Neale, and C. L. Govan, I feel, therefore you act: Interpersonal interpersonal effects of emotion on negotiation as a function of social power. *Organizational Behavior and Human Decision Processes*, 112, 2010: 112–139.

10. Anderson, C. A., and L. Thompson, Affect from the top down: How powerful individuals' positive affect shapes negotiations. *Organizational Behavior and Human Decision Processes*, 95, 2004: 125–139.

11. Kopelman, S., A. Rosette, and L. Thompson, The three faces of Eve: Strategic displays of positive, negative, and neutral emotions in negotiations. *Organizational Behavior and Human Decision Processes*, 99, 2006: 81–101.

12. Lewicki, R. J., Saunders, and Minton, *Negotiation cases and exercise*. New York: McGraw Hill.

TWO

Impression Management: Working the Interview

What others think of you is important. The impression that you make during the interview phase can lay the groundwork for a smooth negotiation process to follow, since a positive impression can lead to an employer's increased willingness to be flexible in the negotiation. In this chapter, we focus upon the ins and outs of successful impression management during the interview process (what works and what doesn't).

Interviews have been described as a crystal ball aiming to show who would be the winners or losers for a particular job opening.[1] But interviews are not just about finding the right person to do the tasks associated with a job; they are also about judging your personality, potential camaraderie, integrity, and compatibility. That's the general list. More specifically, interviewers may also be judging—consciously or unconsciously—whether or not you are the type of person who is any of the following: dependable, fastidious, one with a high intellectual capacity, defensive, thin-skinned, submissive, considerate, one who needs constant reassurance, condescending, warm, willing to face adversity, irritable, etc.[2] In other words, a large part of the interviewer's task is to decide *what you are like as a person*, not just whether or not you can do the job. This, as you can imagine, is a tough assignment, since getting to know what people are really like based on a first impression is nearly impossible to get right. How many of the people whom you later came to respect did you instantly value?

A first impression is essentially what an interview creates, so to successfully navigate the interview, you would be wise to manage the impression that you make. Impression management may not sound like a noble strategy, but it is a tactic actively pursued by savvy job negotiators. Research has shown us that interviewers base their evaluations and recommendations significantly more strongly on their *subjective* impressions of the applicant's interview performance than on the more *objectively* based paper credentials (previous work experience, GPA, etc.).[3]

> **TIP**
>
> Active impression management during the interview is just as critical to the job negotiation as the objective qualifications on your resume.

A GOOD MIND-SET

At the risk sounding like a pep talk, we must state clearly that you need to believe that you can shine brightly in an interview. In the interview context, self-efficacy refers to your ability to truly believe that you have what it takes to do the job. Research shows us that those with this positive mind-set prepare better for their interviews, perform better in the interview itself, and land more job offers than do those who doubt themselves.[4] Fortunately, there are a few tactics that can help you get in, and stay in, a positive frame of mind, which are particularly useful if such a state doesn't come naturally for you. You can remind yourself of other interviews that have gone well, and of other successes that you have had with job assignments or interactions. Try making a list of the skills and talents that you feel will serve your new employer well. Sports psychologists also train athletes to visualize themselves performing perfect actions and winning the event, since this type of mental modeling can actually provide a template for you to act in the real situation. You can similarly visualize yourself as a calm, confident, and competent applicant who is sure to handle the interview with ease and gain the respect of the recruiter. In other words, picture yourself getting the job that you are interviewing for.

These tactics work because they fall under the psychological heading of "internal locus of control," or the idea that when things happen to you, it is because you created them yourself, not simply due to blind luck or someone else's efforts. Keep in mind that those with this high sense of internal control and high self-efficacy feel more empowered to succeed at job-searching, and that this translates directly into both (1) a greater quantity of options and (2) a higher quality of employment outcomes.[5] Lastly, research also reminds us that those who get more interviews and receive more offers are then more confident about their future capabilities,[6] making it that much more critical to have these experiences under your belt because of this upwardly spiraling effect.

TIP

Get into a positive "can-do" frame of mind for your interviews. Try recalling your successes (you wouldn't be invited to the interview at all without prior successes), and mentally visualize yourself succeeding at the job that you are out to get.

WHAT ARE INTERVIEWERS LOOKING FOR?

Most hiring managers take pride in those they are able to recruit, and hope to be hiring the company's next superstar. Generally speaking, those who are hiring tend to look for people whom they feel have good leadership skills (that is, those who are upwardly mobile) and are goal-oriented (that is, those who will deliver results).[7] They are also looking for good communication skills. Despite the widespread and increasing use of computer systems in our professional lives, the basic ability to communicate well, both verbally and in writing, is still important, and you can either get or lose the job offer because of it. In one survey, over 98 percent of hiring interviewers stated that both oral and nonverbal communication skills have a significant impact on hiring decisions.[8] (While we devote an entire chapter to effective communication and persuasion later in this book, here we focus specifically on what interviewers are listening for and what may raise red flags for them.) In this same survey,[9] interviewers reported that the five biggest inadequacies in oral and nonverbal communication that candidates make are:

1. Failure to make eye contact
2. Failure to stay on topic when responding to a question
3. Failure to effectively organize a response (that is, to ramble)
4. Failure to listen effectively
5. Failure to give a clear response

TIP

Look your interviewer in the eye when you speak; give clear, relevant, and organized responses to questions; and listen intently to what is said to you.

Now that we have discussed some of the pitfalls, let's move on to how to actively aim for a positive impression.

MAKING A GOOD IMPRESSION

We know from decades of past research that interviews are *not* actually good tools for predicting how well a prospective employee will do on the job, and yet they remain a mainstay in the job-search process.[10] This is largely because people like the idea that they have the ability to "read" you when they meet and talk to you, and thus can understand your true potential intuitively. This intuition often trumps the sense they get of your future potential from just objectively based written materials, like your resume. Based on this, wise (and ultimately successful) candidates understand the concept of impression management and actively cultivate the kind of first impression that they wish to make on the interviewer, which can lead to bettering the odds of being well received.[11] The research in this area boils down to two main points that can, with delicacy, be utilized to your advantage in making a good impression. The first is about how to present yourself by perfecting your interview stories and addressing your weaknesses; the second is about how to relate to the other person by harnessing the power of similarity.

Presenting Yourself through Stories and Addressing Weaknesses

Ideally, you want to present yourself as being competent, likable, and full of potential. Don't shy away from telling stories about yourself and your successes. In addition to being prepared with good responses to commonly asked interview questions (see the first column of Table 2.1 later in this chapter for a list of likely questions), your own personal anecdotes are an important tool for selling yourself.[12] Even small stories that are not job-related can help the interviewer gain a sense of your confidence. What follows are a list of the four main types of stories that people tend to tell.[13] Hopefully, this list will inspire you to remember some of your own key experiences ahead of the actual interview setting, since you don't want to have to think of these on the fly during the actual interview.

1. Examples of times when you had high levels of responsibility
2. Examples of times when you overcame difficulties, including persuading others who were hard to persuade
3. Positive outcomes you achieved on key tasks
4. Details demonstrating that your success was more rare/unusual than it appears

In fact, the best stories that you can tell cover all four of these areas. You can even organize your story in the order presented above. Start by describing your responsibility for the job or your goal. Move into the challenges faced in the process, describe how you overcame the difficulties and managed people effectively, and how that helped to garner success. Lastly, explain why the success was particularly meaningful for the company.

For example, see the elements at work in the following fictional story:

> In my last job, I was responsible for a team of 10 engineers, each of whom had been in the industry for at least a decade longer than I had. At first they didn't want to listen to the "kid" with the management degree, but I asked them for some leeway to try things my way, and they agreed to give it a shot. I restructured the group into mini-teams with formal consultations with the rest of the group once a week. The team managed to produce three prototypes of new products in a two-month period, two of which went to market within the following 12 months. This was the most productive output for a team of engineers in the company's history.

Select and polish your stories ahead of time. While of course, you don't want to sound like you are giving a speech, a well-rehearsed story is worth the effort. Research has demonstrated that overlearning material means that you will shine even more than normal when asked to perform in front of others, whereas under-learned material may cause you to "choke" in front of others—a tendency called the audience or social facilitation effect.[14] Write down your key stories and experiences ahead of time, then practice them over and over again out loud (in front of the mirror or to a trusted friend, spouse, or colleague, if you can stand it). You won't want to overdo it with too many stories, but instead hone a few anecdotes to demonstrate the best of your past experiences. Remember, interviews can be viewed as a performance just like any other public speaking event, and you can and should require adequate rehearsal from yourself.

TIP

Develop stories to present a picture of who you are. Practice your "stories" and "experiences" over and over again. Out loud and with someone else is best.

To address any potential weaknesses in your record, remember that "the best defense is a good offense." Practicing prepared responses is particularly critical if there is something unusual in your background that is sure to get noticed or might work against you. Extended time off from working? Poor grades? Switching career paths? These elements get noticed, and it is foolish to hope that you will not have to address them. Even if the recruiter doesn't ask, you would be wise to proactively address the issue to head off the potential concern.

A TRUE STORY

Peter was applying for jobs with high expectations but a less-than-stellar GPA. When asked to explain that, he had an answer prepared and well practiced: "As a student I was interested in getting the most out of my education but also exposing myself to multiple responsibilities simultaneously and learning the art of multitasking. I worked at a part-time job throughout school as well as being involved with multiple student groups. These experiences have enabled me to take on public speaking and become involved in various charity programs. Now I have earned my degree and learned an awful lot in my classes, and in addition, I am part of a wide network of organizations, which I think will serve me and my future employer well in the coming years." He was ultimately hired for the job.

The Power of Similarity

Another important aspect of impression management is making the interviewer feel that you are a person who will fit well with the company and, in particular, with your future colleagues. Part of this has to do with how much the interviewer comes to the conclusion, consciously or unconsciously, that "you remind me of *me*!" One of the most fundamental findings in the history of psychology is called the similarity-attraction paradigm, and refers to the idea that we like people who are like us more than we like people who are unlike us.[15] This is an unconscious phenomenon, meaning we tend to do it without realizing it. What is interesting about this is the breadth and depth of the findings—it doesn't matter all that much *how* you are alike: you may look alike, be from the same area, have attended the same schools or—and this is a key one—have similar thoughts and opinions. This phenomenon is so strong, in fact, that people feel closer to, and trust more, their own teammates than members of an opposing team *even if they have never met their teammates*. Being assigned to the "Blue" team makes you rate other "Blue" team members more highly than "Red" team members, even if you don't know anything else about them.[16] This indicates how little it takes for people to feel "on the same team" as each other, and how strong the bond is once you feel this common-team membership, even if it is based on something completely arbitrary.

Placing this into the context of job interviews, this means you want to strive to find ways to make yourself and the interviewer feel similar (and "on the same team"). This can be done by finding background similarities (schooling, hobbies, hometown, etc.), or by knowing somebody in common (even so much as a single person). It also means that the more your opinions conform with the interviewer's, the more likely this person is to rate you as suitable for the job.[17] Now, of course, this does not imply that you should blindly agree with anything the interviewer says—not only could that make you sound silly, but it also might come across as ingratiating, which is not well received on the whole. Instead, just understand that having a common perspective with another person is a tool for building positive feelings about another person. If you can find some sort of connection between yourself and the interviewer, whether done strategically or not, you might just be well on your way to getting the offer.

A TRUE STORY

Danny was thrilled to notice a picture on the hiring manager's wall depicting racehorses, a topic he knew a lot about. He immediately pointed out the picture and made conversation on that topic. It broke the ice, and the rest of the interview felt like a conversation between friends. In retrospect, he was sure that this connection gave him the edge over the competition and resulted in his being hired.

Even if you don't see something obvious to connect on, you can still make a reasonable connection by showing interest in the other person. For instance, if Danny (in the above example) knew nothing of racehorses, he might still have been able to express interest in the topic by commenting, "What a beautiful horse. I've always been interested in horse racing but have not had the chance yet to really explore the sport. Is it a hobby of yours?" Even this can make the person feel like there is a similarity between your interests.

A TRUE STORY

Diana was being interviewed for a job, and the process seemed to be going quite well. The recruiter then began asking her if she knew person after person in the field. Being a relatively new graduate, she had to admit that she did not know any of the people he was listing off. He pursued the topic until he finally named one person whom she knew, albeit indirectly and through her husband's work in a related field. The recruiter instantly and visibly relaxed and seemed to feel that once they knew someone in common, it was now permissible to offer her the job, which he did.

TIP

Find something you share in common with the interviewer and make it salient: similarities can include same schooling, contacts in common, etc.

In fact, this comfort with similar others extends beyond just backgrounds and experiences to even cover one's immediate mood-state or emotions. Research has shown that while people in negative moods tend to share less information with their counterparts and make poorer decisions on the whole, they work better with others and make better decisions if the pair has *matching* moods as opposed to having one positive-mood and one negative-mood partner.[18] In other words, being as similar as possible to the person interviewing you, even on subtle "background" types of cues such as mood, may actually help you both work together more effectively.

THE VALUE OF INTERVIEW EXPERIENCE

While practice may not make perfect, it will ease your jitters. The more interviews you go on, the more job offers you are likely to receive. The number of interviews has been shown to predict the total number of offers—which makes sense because, of course, you cannot receive three offers if you have gone on only two interviews. While interviews are exhausting, nerve-wracking, and uncomfortable, they are well worth the pain and trouble if it increases your odds of landing a desirable job. Plus, even though practicing by going on multiple interviews won't necessarily tell you what you are doing wrong, there is truth in the notion that the more you do something, the less intimidating it becomes, and the more relaxed you are when you do it. In other words, practice will reliably take the edge off your nerves. In addition to practicing your comments and stories before the interview as recommended earlier, you also want to get all the practice you can at actually going to interviews so that the interview process itself begins to feel routine.

A vivid example comes from another context, by way of a woman who conquered her fear of dating by deciding to go out on 100 first dates with the intent of meeting a spouse. Her success at finding the right partner for her was only one of the take-home lessons from her experience. Perhaps the more important one was that after some number of first dates, *they ceased to be anxiety-provoking events* for her. At some point, she just became very good at first dates, and knew what to expect and how to handle it if it was going well or if it wasn't, if she liked the other person or he liked her, or both, or neither.[19] Similarly, the more interviews you go on, the more comfortable you will become with them. Hence, even interviews that you don't expect to result in your dream job can offer something of value to you.

TIP

Go on all the interviews you can. At worst, they are good practice, and at best, you never know when a diamond-in-the-rough job may appear from an opportunity that did not start out as being very promising in the first place.

ASKING GOOD QUESTIONS TO DEMONSTRATE YOUR PASSION

A TRUE STORY

Nicholas knew that the best defense was a good offense. He decided to preempt some tough technical questions by creating his own model for how he thought the business processes ran within the company. When the interview started, he responded to the question of "Why are you interested in this company?" by presenting his model, asking his own follow-up questions, using the manager's whiteboard, and generally impressing the manager. After this, the manager asked a few direct questions, and then the interview was over. He ended up being offered the job.

Preparing means not just knowing how to answer questions, but also how to *ask* engaging questions that demonstrate your true interest in the job. The value of someone who is truly interested in the work is another common theme that we hear from hiring employers. Someone who has interesting and complex questions about the business signals interest in getting *this* job, not just in getting *a* job. See the suggestions in the second column of Table 2.1 to get you started in thinking about questions to ask.[20]

TIP

Most people only focus on preparing their answers to interview questions. Don't forget to also prepare good questions to ask.

Many times we have seen employers skip over objectively better qualified applicants and offer the job to someone who appears to be a less qualified candidate (although meeting their minimum bar), but who has more passion for the company or product. Hiring the "best athlete" model of employment often defers to hiring the "most passionate athlete" when given a choice. Indeed, recruiters repeatedly mention "showing passion for what you do" when asked about what makes a candidate stand out. One business owner said, "I don't care if it's some irrelevant hobby like quilting or stamp collecting, but showing me that you have it in you to really care about things also tells me that you have it in you to be a great employee." Obviously, passion for your profession is even more likely to impress than is passion for your hobbies outside of work. This point is based on the sound psychological principle of intrinsic motivation (IM).

Table 2.1.   Top 10 Common Interview Question Types to Ask and Be Asked[22]

Questions You Might Be Asked	Questions You Might Ask
1. What do you know about this company?	1. What would you like done differently by the next person to hold this position?
2. Why should we hire you? What can you do that someone else can't?	2. What are some of the challenges faced by someone in this position?
3. How does this job fit into your overall career plan? Where do you see yourself in 2–5 years/long term?	3. What are the main objectives for this job? What would you like to see done in the next three months/one year?
4. How would your colleagues/boss describe you?	4. What advancement opportunities might there be from this position?
5. What were the five most significant accomplishments in your last job/in your career?	5. How do you expect the company to grow/change in the foreseeable future/next five years?
6. What are your strengths and weaknesses as an employee? How do you deal with adversity?	6. What are the company's strengths and weaknesses?
7. What would you expect to accomplish in the first year at this job?	7. How is performance evaluated in this role?
8. Why are you looking to change jobs? What do you look for in a job?	8. What skills do you not already have on board that you are looking for?
9. What do you think is the most difficult part of being a manager/supervisor?	9. How does this job fit in with the overall structure and goals of this company?
10. How would you describe your leadership/management style? Your work style? What motivates you?	10. What have been some of the organization's biggest successes?

As opposed to those who are motivated by external forces such as money, people who are high in IM are the types who get wholly absorbed in what they do and find pleasure in it for its own sake. Needless to say, these people tend to produce more creative outcomes in their work than those who are merely working toward the bottom line.[21] If you give the impression that you are the type who does your job just to get it done and collect a paycheck, you will probably be crossed off the list.

TIP

Show passion for your work.

INTERVIEW FAQ

Should I Smile a Lot?

Candidates generally smile more than interviewers do, which supports the idea that smiling reflects lower status. Research has shown that male interviewers tend to smile less than female ones, and less than the candidate.[23] Keep in mind that the goal is to come across as warm and friendly but still competent and intelligent, so plastering a false smile on your face is probably not necessary, but maintaining a positive and confident mood is, which may entail some smiles.

What Should I Wear?

Ideally, you will want to know ahead of time the dress code for the place you would like to work, and then be either the same or one level more formal than the average employee. Being underdressed is a greater sin than being overdressed in general. However, coming dressed in a full suit when the employees wear jeans risks having you come across as a potentially poor fit for the company's culture (or even give the impression that you are overqualified). Ideally, as part of your preparation for the interview, you will have a chance to ask this type of question to someone (other than your interviewer) already working for the company. Early research in this area also observed that for women, dressing in a more "masculine" style (that is, conservative suits) led to better evaluations for management positions than dressing in more feminine ways.[24] Overall, you don't want your clothing to stand out in any obvious way—the goal is to make that a nonissue, allowing the real substance of your abilities and qualifications to shine through.

One exception to this rule is in a situation such as a career fair, where having something unique about your visual presentation can make people remember you. One female student tells of wearing a white suit and noted that when she later went in for several interviews, many people commented, "I remember you; you were the one in the white suit."

Lastly, people sometimes ask about whether it makes sense to wear eyeglasses or not in an interview, and the answer is that it depends what type of job you are interviewing for. Research has shown that candidates are more likely to be hired for managerial jobs with glasses, and for sales positions without glasses.[25] This is because people who wear glasses are thought to be more intelligent, industrious, and dependable, and interviewers link these personality traits to some types of jobs more than others. There are also gender differences in the effect of eyeglasses, as male candidates who wear glasses are labeled as charismatic, capable, and handsome, while female candidates are labeled as sociable, reliable, and attractive.

Is There a Disadvantage to Being Interviewed over the Phone Rather Than in Person?

Phone interviews generally fall into the category of structured interviews in which interviewers ask the same questions to all interviewees. There is typically little opportunity for follow-ups, and assessment is done on a standardized rating form. Companies like them because, in addition to the efficiencies associated with trying to make decisions without the time and expense of bringing all candidates in for on-site meetings, they can ask scripted questions and fill out rating forms without the candidates' awareness. But, research shows that candidates tend to be *less prepared* and *less focused* for these interviews. People may not psych themselves up as intensely for a phone call as they do for a face-to-face meeting. That is, you may not get into full "interview mode" for a phone interview in part because perhaps you are at home and in something very casual like jeans and a T-shirt instead of work clothing. There is also a greater chance of interruptions or distractions taking place while at home (children, call-waiting, etc.).[26]

On the other hand, for some well-prepared candidates, communicating via phone has some advantages. Hidden from sight, this candidate can have "cheat sheets" about the company, lists of questions to ask, scripted responses, and the like all laid out on paper in plain view for easy reference. Materials such as these can even be used in video interviews if strategically placed out of sight of the camera.

In contrast to phone interviews, in unstructured face-to-face interviews, there is a free-flowing exchange of ideas in which complex questions are encouraged. When candidates do have the opportunity to talk more in the unstructured interview, they tend to be more behaviorally expressive, and so this tends to yield more accurate personality judgments.[27] People in face-to-face interviews perceive candidates to be more cheerful, warm, considerate, and socially at ease on the whole. This happens because personality traits that are typically conveyed via nonverbal behavior get lost on the phone, and because phone interviews tend to be shorter in general and with fewer follow-up questions asked by both sides, thus leading to less information being exchanged in total.[28]

With proper preparation and the right attitude, this means that the face-to-face format is the better one to win over the interviewer. One manager said, "You won't *get* the job on the phone, but you can *lose* the job on the phone. I need to hear that you have some basic (technical) competence, are personable, and come across as the person I imagined from reading your resume. After that we need to meet face-to-face." Another said, "Never talk money on the phone. Don't ask a lot of questions on the phone. Just get me to the want-to-meet-you phase and you have done all you can on the phone." Yet some companies try to do the entire interview process over the phone, to save on interview expenses. If you are serious about the job, you may want to try to meet in person if possible, and at your own expense if necessary. If you are a prepared candidate who can leave a positive impression, then push for the face-to-face interview whenever possible. The phone just does not do you justice.

What Do I Need to Know about Where and How to Sit in the Interview?

While you will most likely be shown to a seat, there are a few things worth knowing about the science of proxemics, or how our closeness to other people sends various signals. Though this is culturally determined to a large degree, U.S. culture dictates that business associates should interact anywhere from 4 to 12 feet away from each other. Closer than that tends to feel uncomfortable for someone who is not family or a close friend, and further than that feels too distant. In terms of seating dynamics, sitting beside someone can trigger cues of cooperation between the two, whereas sitting across a table or desk from someone may feel more competitive. Open and direct communication is best facilitated by sitting across the corner of a desk or table from each other and so is probably the best option, if you are fortunate enough to be given a choice of where to sit during the interview conversation.[29]

Is There Anything I Should NEVER Say in an Interview?

Yes! There are, of course, plenty of "don't go there" topics for interview dialogue, starting with any kind of curse, off-color language, or reference to anything illegal. As we list below, most of the rest are similarly based on common sense, with one exception.

- Don't say that you are unsure about wanting the job, unless you are positive you don't want the offer. Similarly, don't come across as indifferent about your career as a whole (for example, interviewing for a position at a law firm and reporting that you had become a lawyer only because your mother wanted you to and you actually didn't care one way or the other).

- Don't discuss any health-related matters. (This includes questions about drug-testing procedures!)
- Don't complain about a former workplace or former colleagues.

And the one item that may not be obvious without being told:

- Steer the conversation away from specific salary information—whether it is your current/prior salary or your expected salary (more on this in Chapter 3). Simply put, don't discuss your salary at the interview.

How Do I Overcome My Nerves?

The best answer for this is the one we have already discussed: practice, practice, practice. And then practice some more. Practice your stories and experiences and answers to common questions before you get to the interview, and practice going on actual interviews as often as possible.

But there is also another tactic to add to the list that's tremendously effective. That is *pretending to be someone else*—more specifically, someone whom you admire and who is confident and qualified for the job in question. Research shows that this tactic can help overcome even the worst bouts of anxiety and free you up to stay calm, read the situational cues better, and communicate more effectively.[30] Similarly, this also works when you get to the actual negotiation stage of the hiring process; pretending that you are negotiating on someone else's behalf tends to make you much more bold about making requests and voicing concerns.

Is There Anything I Should Pay Special Attention to during My Office Visit?

Most obviously, you will need to learn what the job entails and whether it is both of interest to you and within your skill set. In addition to your interview, your office visit will allow you to better observe the culture firsthand in that particular firm. Of course, you learn a lot by talking to people and asking direct questions, but you will also learn a lot by observation alone. The way people dress tells you how formal the company is, as does the way people address each other (whether it is a "Mr. So-and-So" type of culture, or one in which the CEO insists on being called Chris). Where and how do people eat lunch—in their cubicles alone, or out at the local diner? Or, if there's a company cafeteria, how do people sit—is it strictly by department or rank, or is there a lot of mixing? Do executives eat separately from other employees (such as in a private dining room), or with their subordinates? Even the physical layout of the office itself can tell you about the values of the organization. All of these will give you clues as to the potential fit between yourself and the employer, and are best uncovered during your office interview.

In addition, there are likely a number of potential benefits to working for one firm over another that you may find out about during your office visit. While they might not be negotiable, nor should they be the focus of any of your interviews (because you don't want to seem too focused on the nonwork elements of the job), they are things that you might want to keep your eyes open for (or ask the HR rep instead of the hiring manager, if possible). A non-exhaustive list of benefits that enhance one's quality of life includes:

- Tuition reimbursement
- Professional organization membership and events
- Day care
- Athletic/country club membership or facilities on-site
- Legal, financial planning, and/or CPA tax assistance
- Product discounts
- Short-term loans
- Company car or automobile lease
- Environmental friendliness, and the potential for bonuses for either developing new environmentally friendly ideas or giving up your parking space and carpooling or biking when possible
- Wellness programs, including stress reduction classes, healthy food and vending options, or even access to filtered water

SPECIAL TOPIC: GENDER AND RACIAL BIAS IN JOB NEGOTIATIONS

Needless to say, the world is not yet equal for all, and inequality can arise in interviews and job negotiations. For example, data from the Bureau of Labor Statistics clearly demonstrates that salary disparities continue to exist between men and women to this very day. Women earn, on average, 80 cents for every dollar paid to men. Statistically speaking, blacks and Hispanics make about 76 cents on the dollar as compared to whites. And in the past, as the percentage of women and minorities in an industry increased, the weekly salaries for that industry decreased, while the opposite happened for white men.[31] One explanation for the gender part of this trend is that jobs thought of as traditionally "women's work" often just pay less than those that are considered "men's work." As an example, even when they decide to become doctors, women flock in disproportionate numbers to specialties involving other women and children (pediatrics and obstetrics/gynecology), which pay less than other specialties such as surgery. However, some of the difference is also based on women receiving less pay for *identical* work as compared to men.

There is also evidence that racial biases may manifest themselves in job negotiations. One of the toughest aspects of racial bias in job interviews and negotiations is that so much of it is unconscious. Company recruiters, of course, do not feel that they are being biased against a candidate, but some interesting psychological experiments demonstrate that they are often biased nonetheless, albeit unconsciously. For example, one study showed different groups of people identical resumes with two simple changes.[32] One set of resumes had a name typically associated with someone who is white, while the other had a name typically associated with someone who is black. The second change was that half of each set of resumes showed a candidate strong on experience but lacking in solid educational background, while the other showed a candidate strong on education but lacking in real-world experience. One group of people compared these two resumes: Person A was white with good experience, while Person B was black with good education. Another group of people compared the opposite two possibilities: Person A was white with good education, while Person B was black with good experience. Now, here's where it gets interesting: *both* sets of people overwhelmingly chose the candidate with the white-sounding name, but gave *different* reasons for having done so. In the first group, people justified their decision by saying that experience was so much more important than education. In the second group, people gave rationales that spoke of how important a good education was, and that experience could always be earned over time. Nobody thought that they were being biased, but the consistent switch in logic demonstrated otherwise.

A TRUE STORY

Priya tried an experiment during a job search. She posted two different versions of her resume, one with her own Indian name and another, identical in content, with a Western-sounding name on it instead. She was shocked and dismayed to find that while she did get responses from both versions, they were for different job types:

her Indian name got her calls for technical jobs, and her Western name got her calls for management jobs.

Similarly, disturbing research has also shown that people may evaluate performance, such as how you did in a job interview, differently depending on skin color. For example, research shows that when people had to evaluate the performance of one of three sales clerks of different races (work examples were portrayed on a video, and performance was objectively identical), people tended to rate the white male the highest, which the researchers attributed to an unconscious bias that favors white males.[33] In the interview context, experiments have also shown that white interviewers tend to speak more poorly and act less enthusiastically with black candidates than with white ones, leading to a potentially negative spiral of events in which the minority candidate then becomes less confident and performs less well in the interview.[34]

Some research has shown that women and racial minorities may also negotiate less effectively for both their starting salaries and their raises.[35] In the case of women, this may perhaps be due to their socialization to value a more relationship-based style of interaction, thus encouraging them to settle for less in an effort to not endanger the relationship. Though there is also some evidence that women receive less *even when they ask for the same amount* as men,[36] the bigger (and fortunately, the more correctable) problems are that they either (1) do not ask at all, and are too quick to assume that their good work will instead be rewarded at a future point; or (2) force themselves to be too demanding in an attempt to demonstrate that they are as tough as their male counterparts. There is some good news too, though. Women may be better equipped for thinking outside the box to get both their own needs and the needs of the other side met in negotiations. And everyone can improve their outcomes, even despite situational disadvantages, by learning about negotiations and effectively preparing for them, as we aim to teach in this book.

Overcoming Gender and Racial Biases

Unfortunately, if you are a minority (whether gender or racial), the burden is on *you* to make your case, as explicitly as possible, about your qualifications and why *you* are the right one for the job. Is this fair? No, but it is reality. Minority candidates in particular need to be better prepared and able to sell themselves effectively. Our advice is that you should assume that no employer intentionally wants to be biased or to discriminate in regard to gender or race, which is generally a true assumption. But, let's face it: the empirical data strongly suggest that there are unconscious, and hence unintentional, biases that can potentially manifest themselves during the interview process. Here are seven suggested approaches to interviews and job negotiations with an eye toward minimizing the gender and racial biases that may arise. Pick and choose the ones that may work best for your particular situation.

1. Understand that interviews and negotiations are triggers for gender and racial inequality, and go in prepared.[37]

2. Use your networks. *Personal* connections can help overcome these blind-bias issues. (Recall the tip about commonality made earlier in this chapter).

3. Set high goals. Respectfully force someone to have to say no.

4. Recollect yourself if someone says no, and respectfully continue to keep the issues on the table.

5. Do not downplay your accomplishments.

6. Be yourself. Learn the science of job negotiations, but use your personal style. Do not adopt a negotiation style that does not reflect who you are.[38]

7. If all else fails and you feel intimidated, imagine that you are negotiating on someone else's behalf.

SUMMARY

The impression that you present from the moment you first make contact with your future employer will influence the job negotiation. Given this, proactively manage it to your advantage. Be aware of potential pitfalls to impression management and take steps to counteract them. Practice for the job interview to ensure that you project a positive image by preparing and rehearsing your stories, your answers to their probable questions, and your own questions that you have for them. Such practice will not only make you more comfortable, but every interview you participate in will also give you better odds at landing the right offer. Find (and express!) the things you may have in common with the interviewer. For impression management to succeed, it is crucial to believe that you are the right person for this job and to stay in a positive frame of mind.

NOTES

1. Farrell, B. M., Recruitment: The art and success of employment interviews. *Personnel Journal*, 65, 1986: 91–94.

2. Blackman, M., Personality judgment and the utility of the unstructured employment interview. *Basic and Applied Social Psychology*, 24, 2002: 241–250.

3. Stevens, C. K., and A. L. Kristof, Making the right impression: A field study of applicant impression management during job interviews. *Journal of Applied Psychology*, 80, 1995: 587–606.

4. Kanfer, R. and L. Hulin, Individual differences in successful job searches following lay-off. *Personnel Psychology*, 38, 1985: 835–847.

5. Moynihan, L. M., et al., A longitudinal study of the relationships among job search self-efficacy, job interviews, and employment outcomes. *Journal of Business Psychology*, 18, 2003: 207–233.

6. Tay, C., S. Ang, and L. Van Dyne, Personality, biographical characteristics, and job interview success: A longitudinal study of the mediating effects of interviewing self-efficacy and the moderating effects of internal locus of causality. *Journal of Applied Psychology*, 91, 2006: 446–545.

7. Rynes, S., and B. Gerhart, Interviewer assessments of applicant "fit": An exploratory investigation. *Personnel Psychology*, 43, 1990: 13–35.

8. Peterson, M. S., Personnel interviewers' perceptions of the importance and adequacy of applicants' communication skills. *Communication Education*, 46, 1997: 287–291.

9. Ibid.

10. Arvey, R. C., and J. E. Campion, The employment interview: A summary and review of recent research. *Personnel Psychology*, 51, 1998: 845–848.

11. Ferris, G. R., and T. A. Judge, Personnel/human resources management: A political influence perspective. *Journal of Management*, 17, 1991: 447–488.

12. http://www.careercc.com and http://www.careerbuilder.com, 2010.

13. Stevens and Kristof, Making the right impression.

14. Zajonc, R. B., Social facilitation. *Science*, 149, 1965: 269–274.

15. Byrne, D., *The attraction paradigm*. New York: Academic Press, 1971.

16. Tajfel, H., and J. C. Turner, The social identity theory of intergroup behavior. In *Psychology of intergroup relations*, S. Worchel and W. G. Austin, Editors. Chicago: Nelson-Hall, 1986.

17. Stevens and Kristof, Making the right impression.

18. Levin, D. Z., T. R. Kurtzberg, K. W. Phillips, and R. B. Lount, The role of mood in knowledge transfer and learning. *Group Dynamics: Theory, Research, and Practice*, 14, 2010: 123–142.

19. Marsh, A., What I learned from dating 100 men. In *O, the Oprah Magazine*, February 2003.

20. http://www.careercc.com and http://www.careerbuilder.com, 2010.

21. Amabile, T., *Creativity in context*. Boulder, CO: Westview Press, 1996.

22. http://www.careercc.com and http://www.careerbuilder.com, 2010.

23. Deutsch, F. M., Status, sex, and smiling: The effect of smiling in men and women. *Personality and Social Psychology Bulletin*, 16(3), 1990: 531–540.

24. Forsythe, S., M. F. Drake, and C. E. Cox, Influence of applicant's dress on interviewer's selection decisions. *Journal of Applied Psychology*, 70, 1985: 374–378.

25. Lusnar, M. P., Job applicant stereotypes: Effects of eyeglasses and job type in a simulated interview. *Dissertation Abstracts International: Section B: The Sciences and Engineering*, 60(2-B), 1999: 2.

26. Blackman, M., The employment interview via the telephone: Are we sacrificing accurate personality judgments for cost efficiency? *Journal of Research in Personality*, 35, 2002: 208–223.

27. Blackman, Personality judgment and the utility of the unstructured employment interview.

28. Blackman, The employment interview via the telephone.

29. Nelson, D. L., and J. C. Quick, *Organizational behavior: Foundations, realities, and challenges*. 4th ed. Australia: Thomson-Southwestern, 2003.

30. Hirsch, C. R., et al., Interview anxiety: Taking the perspective of a confident other changes inferential processing. *Behavioural and Cognitive Psychotherapy*, 33, 2005: 1–12.

31. Boraas, S., and W. Rodgers, How gender influences the earnings gap. *Bureau of Labor Statistics Monthly Labor Review*, 2003.

32. Stockdale, M., and F. Crosby, *The psychology and management of workplace diversity*. Hoboken, NJ: Blackwell Publishing, 2003.

33. Heckman, D. R., et al., *An examination of whether and how racial and gender biases influence customer satisfaction*. Academy of Management Journal, in press.

34. Word, C. O., M. P. Zanna, and J. Cooper, The nonverbal mediation of self-fulfilling prophecies in interracial interaction. *Journal of Experimental Social Psychology*, 10, 1974: 109–120.

35. Babcock, L., and S. Laschever, *First you have to ask*, in *Negotiation*, 2004: 3–5. Cambridge, MA: Harvard Law School.

36. Juodvalkis, J. L., et al., The effects of job stereotype, applicant gender, and communication style on ratings in screening interviews. *International Journal of Organizational Analysis*, 11, 2003: 67–84.

37. Pradel, D. W., H. R. Bowles, and K. L. McGinn, *When gender changes the negotiation*, in *HBS Working Knowledge*. 2006, Cambridge, MA: Harvard Business School.

38. Flexo, Negotiating for salary: Men vs. women. In *Consumerism Commentary*, 2005.

THREE

Beginning the Negotiation: When to Start, and When *Not* To

In addition to knowing when you should start negotiating your employment terms, you also need to know when *not* to negotiate. Though they often blend in practice, it is best to keep the interview phase separate from the negotiation phase. All too often, we see specific terms (such as salary figures) being brought up for discussion before any offer of employment is extended. This chapter explores this aspect of the job negotiation process and puts aside any ambiguity about *when* the negotiation should ideally begin and what you should do, and should not do, before that point. In essence, we strongly recommend that you avoid jumping into the actual discussion of employment details too early, and by too early, we mean before a written offer is extended. If you start negotiating before this point, the potential losses you face typically outweigh any potential gains. The losses usually occur when you, the candidate, anchor the negotiation in the wrong place by saying the wrong first number, thus limiting the value you may have gotten out of the deal, or even prematurely eliminating yourself for consideration for the job. We will walk through the details of this process, but the guiding principle throughout this chapter is that you generally want the company, your potential future employer, to present their offer with their numbers first.

GETTING A *WRITTEN* OFFER

As far as the job negotiation goes, you should consider the interview phase as simply setting the stage for the job negotiation to occur. The optimal culmination of the interview stage is that you are presented with a formal written job offer—not a *verbal* offer, but a *written* one. You do not want to start negotiating your employment terms (or worse, accept the offer as is) until *after* you get an offer in writing. Note that a while a formal written contract is best, even an informal e-mail summarizing the main elements of the offer is far better than spoken words alone. If an offer is extended to you verbally, which frequently happens, we suggest that you thank them with sincerity for the offer, state that you are excited about the possibility of working with them, and respectfully inquire about when you will get the offer in writing so that you can go over it (and examine the details, review it with your spouse, etc.). *Once the written offer is in your hands, the job negotiation can begin.*

In the course of a spoken conversation with your future employer (whether face-to-face or over the telephone) it may feel very tempting to simply say "yes" to a verbal offer. After all, the company representative will be waiting for your response to gauge your interest. You are probably also interested, given that you have gotten to this point. Both sides are anxious to bring the matter to a successful close. But even if the offer is an attractive one and will likely be accepted regardless, we still highly recommend that you get that offer in writing before providing acceptance, for two reasons. First, it protects you against the possibility that the terms of employment may suddenly shift (for example, "we really had this in mind when we offered you the job"). With a written contract, you have evidence of the terms of employment offered, and it is difficult for the company to follow up a written offer with a "worse" package. But verbal offers are very easy to change, often for the worse, and can be rescinded with no consequences. Keep in mind that written employment contracts are legal documents and can be enforced (while verbal offers have no legal backing). Even without any intention of forcing legal actions, written employment offers are taken more seriously than verbal offers by all parties. Second, not accepting a verbal offer allows you the opportunity to consider the various options or generate potential alternatives away from the emotional "heat" generated during a person-to-person interaction. In fact, it may allow you to relax more during the entire conversation, knowing that you will not be giving your final answer right away no matter what is offered.

Waiting to get an offer in writing before providing acceptance is a good idea, even if it is the best offer you had hoped to get. Fortunately, it is standard practice at companies with a human resource department (or similar) to give a written offer when extending the opportunity for employment. But not all—it may truly be a company's practice to get a verbal commitment before proceeding to the paperwork. This is more typically true in small firms than in large ones, but it can happen anywhere. It could also signal that something is not quite right—for example, the company may be keeping their options open, or may have less-than-admirable plans for how to proceed with your package (we have seen both of these and highlight some examples in the stories below). Refusal to give a written offer of employment terms is generally a warning flag, and can go badly for you in a number of ways.

FOUR TRUE STORIES

Bill had an excellent interview with his company's chief technology officer, and during the course of the discussion, he was offered a very attractive package. The two shook hands and agreed to a deal. When Bill went in later to sign the official paperwork, the deal was not even close to the same as the one he was promised, and he found that the verbal agreement was no longer honored. In his words, "the CTO knew he had me at that point" and he took the job anyway, but with lesser compensation and greater animosity.

Similarly, Abby was offered a job package that she verbally accepted only to find the person who offered her the job was fired soon after her acceptance. The new recruiter changed a number of details in the employment contract when it was finally presented. Although Abby turned down the revised written offer, she nonetheless lost over two months of her time that could have been spent interviewing at other companies.

Carmen was overqualified for the position she was interviewing for, but in a tough economy, she decided the opportunity was worth it for her anyway, as a better opportunity was not forthcoming. The company gave her a verbal offer and asked for a response after the weekend. Having taken one of our classes, she wisely asked for a written contract and a reasonable period of time to consider it, and was told that written offers were not issued until a verbal commitment was made. She asked if that was standard procedure at this company, and was told only, "We like it this way." She wasn't comfortable with the whole process and declined the verbal offer, and then found out later that they didn't want to tie up the position with formal paperwork on her since they thought she would say no anyway. She was glad she had passed on a company that would act that way, though she would have accepted the offer otherwise.

Lastly, Gabe was a successful MBA specializing in commercial real estate. Unfortunately, when the commercial real estate market took a turn for the worse, his firm went under. No other firms were hiring, and so he struck a verbal deal with the partner of an existing firm that had a lot of small (essentially one-room) vacant office spaces to fill. Gabe could fill the empty spaces for a commission on the rent that was charged. An innovative salesperson, he filled up a considerable number of vacant offices and was expecting a six-figure cut (to be paid quarterly). When it came time to be paid, he was surprised that his check was for only about 10 percent of what he expected. He confronted the partner with whom he had made the deal, only to realize that they had each (verbally) agreed to different deals. The partner's expectation was that the commission would be paid on any extra offices leased that were above the forecasted budget. Gabe's interpretation was that it would be a commission on all the units he filled (with no consideration of what was forecasted or budgeted). With no written contract to support him, all he could do was cut his losses. He quit.

TIP

Do not accept or negotiate a verbal offer. Have a written offer in hand before negotiating.

WHY YOU DON'T WANT TO STATE THE FIRST NUMBER

Realistically, you do need to be prepared for the fact that a notable number of employers prefer to deal explicitly with job package details during the interview process. Even written applications for jobs (in hard copy or online) often contain questions such as "What is your desired salary range?" or "What is your current salary?" Many employers or HR departments do this strategically in order to weed out people from a large pool of candidates. You will want to acknowledge the importance of such questions, but tactfully and respectfully avoid giving any details as to your desires or bottom line. Most of the time, these uncomfortable questions focus specifically on base salary—your past salary, current salary, salary expectations, etc. Sometimes it is asked out loud in a series of blunt, direct questions such as "What salary did you have in mind?" or "What do you currently make?" We know your instinct will be to give an answer of some kind, but we suggest that you push this salary conversation off until you have a written offer from them first (and we will address specifically how to head off these types of questions a little further into this chapter).

Avoiding salary questions protects you along a couple of fronts. It can protect you from being eliminated from consideration for a particular job (because your salary expectations are either too high or too low), and it can protect you from being offered a lower salary than the employer may have been willing to offer otherwise. In other words, once you say a number, you will likely not get much more than that number, so you have effectively capped all future salary negotiations with your own figure, even if there might have been room for higher numbers to be offered. On top of that, most people undervalue themselves and ask for too little. And on occasion, even if you have provided a low number from the company's perspective, you may still get bargained down a bit further. Some companies believe that this will actually make you feel better about your final contract (since people are generally less satisfied with deals when their first offer is accepted rather than counter-bid), when in truth the objective value of your package was just cut by an even greater amount.

If you went to sell a piece of jewelry, it is considered "entrapment" for the jeweler to ask *you* what price you wanted, when it was instead the jeweler's job to make you an offer for your goods. On the job negotiation front, though it is certainly legal for the company to ask you what you would like to make (or what you already earn), it puts you at a disadvantage for the same types of reasons. Additionally, you should be aware that in a job negotiation, the salary number is really just one element of the deal that should not be discussed in isolation but is instead part of a larger package. Delaying the conversation until you have a complete written offer including all employment terms allows you to have more flexibility in moving the salary number around to appropriately reflect other aspects of the deal that might be more or less appealing to you. Generally speaking, during the interview process, your overall objective is to get them to want to hire you and thus extend an offer of employment to you. Get the job offer, get it in writing, and then start to negotiate.

TIP

Avoid spoken discussion of specific details regarding employment terms during the interview phase—especially details regarding salary.

People who do decide to mention specific salary numbers are, in effect, rolling the dice. That is to say, sometimes you can hit it big, while other times it may severely limit the amount you might otherwise have been offered. It's incredibly hard to know which way it will fall ahead of time, as the following stories illustrate.

FIVE TRUE STORIES

Rachel didn't really want the job she was interviewing for, and so when they asked her what kind of salary she was looking for, she said the biggest number she could think of, and was shocked when they replied that they could do that for her.

But also consider Louis, who told the interviewer the details of another high-level offer that he had, only to have the interviewer stand up and say, "Congratulations. Take their offer."

Allison asked for a high number and was passed over because the company assumed that she was overqualified if that was the salary she was commanding for the job.

Then again, there was Wyatt, who said a specific salary number (X) and was told by the interviewer that the company had a range that started above that number so the offer would be X + 15%. He walked out wondering how much further the range actually extended.

Finally, there was Amy, who put down a written response to the "desired salary range" on the application form and had the interviewer ask her point-blank "That's a really high number, do you really expect to get that?"

All of these people gambled at the numbers game; some won and some lost. Through this book, we would like you to learn how to make the most of your job negotiation opportunity. This means stacking the deck in your favor when dealing with one of the most sensitive issues in the job negotiation: money.

Yet one last reason to avoid mentioning salary numbers prior to getting a written offer is the potential impact of emotions. Emotions can run high during job-related conversations such as interviews, which may cloud your judgment in the moment and may lead you to put forth a salary number that is not to your advantage. It is reasonable to assume that you, as the candidate for a job, are likely to be more nervous and emotional about the whole process than is the hiring recruiter, because of the greater importance the outcome holds for your life than for that of the recruiter. However, research also shows that emotions tied to this heightened sense of importance can have unintended effects on your decision making. The emotion-based "How do I feel about it?" method of deciding on an offer, as opposed to the more cognitive and calculated "What's a reasonable offer?" method, can lead you to concede more to the other side before you have even heard their offer. Why? Because you may talk yourself into being afraid of the other side's reaction to your request, and adjust (downward) accordingly. In other words, people sometimes sell themselves short because they are afraid that the other side would react badly to the number that they had hoped to put forth.[1]

ANCHORING AGAINST YOUR OWN BEST INTERESTS

Many people have heard that they should anchor negotiations whenever they can by stating the first number. Yet our advice here is specifically to *avoid* being the one to state the first number. Why? By way of explanation, we will start with a description of what anchoring is and how it works. Anchoring refers to the tendency for people to remain rooted to whatever number or idea is presented first. Once people hear any number, even an obviously irrelevant one, it will likely anchor their thinking, or pull their own numerical estimates towards that point. For example, we ask our students to estimate how many rats there are in New York City. We tell one class that my grandmother, who has never been to New York and knows nothing about rats, thinks there might be 10,000 rats. In a second class, we tell the students that my grandmother estimated that there might be 25,000 rats. In all likelihood, the students in the first class would guess numbers that are closer to 10,000 than to 25,000, and vice versa for the second class. Even though they were told that my grandmother's guess was uninformed, it can be hard to "unring the bell" and ignore the anchoring effect of the stated number.

This decision-making bias, called anchoring, makes it seem as if you want to be the one to jump in and offer that first number. After all, research on negotiations has shown that final settlement values are more closely related to first offers than to any other element in the whole negotiation, and those who make first offers on the whole do better in their final outcome.[2] In job negotiations, as in other negotiations, the first number stated has the potential to act like an anchor; hence, the first offer is indeed a critical element in the negotiation. But the power of your being the one to anchor a job negotiation also comes laced with danger. The first number you say, should it be the wrong one, can anchor the whole job negotiation in the wrong direction, as we have seen many times and was portrayed in some of the earlier examples. The numbers that you have spent time thinking about, whether it be your current salary, your goal salary, or someone else's salary, can all serve as (misguided) anchors as well and drive you to waste this powerful opportunity with a number to your disadvantage.

TWO TRUE STORIES

Robin was entering an industry where she knew several other current professionals, each earning about $125,000 a year. Entering her negotiation, she was focused on that number and was shocked, and even a little insulted, when the final offer for her came in at only $110,000 a year. Though she turned down the job, she was later sorry as she realized that there were reasonable explanations for the difference, such as the fact that most other firms demanded an 80-hour-plus work week and tons of travel, whereas her particular firm did not.

On the other side, Randy was focused entirely on his pre-MBA salary of $65,000. A new offer for $85,000 seemed fantastic to him, and he took it without hesitation. He hadn't given due consideration, however, to whether this was an appropriate salary number to be discussing, and he later realized that even this number was below the industry norm.

As a job candidate, anchoring can throw off reasoned thinking, and it is important to account for its effects. This is why good, solid, quality information about what salary range you should expect is critical, coupled with an understanding of what your own market worth really is.

TIP

Generally speaking, don't try to anchor your job negotiation. The side with better information should be the one to say the first number. In the majority of job negotiation situations, this is the company, not the candidate.

AVOIDING THE SALARY CONVERSATION, SPECIFICALLY

Even if you take our advice and do not start negotiating before receiving a written offer, this will not necessarily stop your recruiter from probing for your salary history and preferences. In fact, some may press you quite directly on this information. Thus, it helps to have some tactics under your belt to address this situation, and to do so respectfully. We offer four general points to redirect salary questions. First, many companies will ask you to fill out a form on your way in to the interview. On most of these forms, there is an innocent-looking box labeled "desired salary range" for you to fill out. Being a conscientious professional, your instinct is probably to fill out every line on a form. On the contrary, we advise that you *leave that spot blank* and wait to see if the interviewer raises the issue in conversation. Once you are in the interview itself, we recommend that you use the Noel Smith-Wenkle Salary Negotiation Method (named after the headhunter who developed the system) to push that sensitive salary conversation off until later.[3] To use this method, memorize the following three sentences.

Response 1. The first time they ask you how much you'll take, reply:
"I am much more interested in doing (type of work) here at (name of company) than I am in the size of the *initial* offer."

Here, you haven't limited any future discussion on monetary compensation, but instead have refocused the conversation on the job itself. Noel says that about 40 percent of the time this comment is all you need. However, if they ask you again, move on to Response 2.

Response 2. The second time they ask, reply:
"I will *consider* any *reasonable* offer."

Note that you really have not offered any substantive information here, other than that you would like the employer to make the first offer. It is their job, and so they should know what a reasonable offer looks like. Noel said that in only about 30 percent of the cases, interviewers stayed focused on this topic. If they do, move on to the final option.

Response 3. If they push, a third delay tactic would be to reply:
"You are in a much better position to know how much I'm worth to you than I am."

Again, without being impolite, you have tossed the ball back into their court for the first offer.

What if the interviewer simply will not proceed without you discussing either (1) what you currently earn, or (2) what you hope to earn? That can certainly happen. The majority of HR people that we have consulted with have admitted that when candidates opt out of the salary conversation, they are willing to let it drop as well. But some say they simply will not proceed without that information, because it is standard procedure for them to get that before they allow the interview to continue. A loose rule of thumb is that the higher up you go in terms of position and title, the more they are going to want to use a "current salary plus" pricing strategy to determine your offer. Consequently, they are anchoring on what you already make. But, in addition to your current salary number, don't forget that market rates, and/or the salaries of others doing the same type of work, can be equally persuasive, so you might be able to shift the focus from your salary to one of these. Another option in these cases is for you to justify why the current salary amount is not a relevant figure for discussion. For example, perhaps you are switching industries, or you now have a higher degree or other qualifications or more experience than you had before. These reasons, ideally offered without an actual salary number (but work well even if you do need to report a salary number), should help steer the conversation away from that number as an anchoring point and toward the current opportunity instead.

Even more problematic are the websites (either company-specific application pages or generalist job-search engines) that require you to enter a value for one or both of these questions before you are permitted to submit your application. Then what? Our advice is to think about how much this opportunity is worth to you, knowing that filling in that number is likely to put you at a disadvantage for any subsequent job negotiations with that company. You could also consider putting a ridiculously low number (we have seen candidates put in salary numbers such as $10 and still proceed to get an interview). Only you can decide whether it's worth it to proceed, but at least you can go in with your eyes open.

SHOULD YOU *ALWAYS* LET THEM MAKE THE FIRST OFFER?

The answer here goes back to the value of good information on what the job is worth, and what the company might be willing to offer you. If you have *very good* information on what the job is worth, then it might be to your advantage to offer a number near or at the very top of their range. But, you need to be sure that your information is both current and accurate. Even well-researched salary numbers can be wrong if you do not have perfect information.

A TRUE STORY

Anna was currently working at a job that paid about $100,000, but for many reasons (location, stability, etc.) was considering a lateral move to a similar job with a less well-off company. She had a good friend who worked for the new company, and he had been signed a few years back at about $75,000. With raises, he was now making a bit over $80,000 for the same job description she was interviewing for. With this information, Anna decided that she should anchor the negotiation in her favor by telling the interviewer her current salary. To her surprise, the interviewer, without batting an eye, told her that they could meet her at that figure. Suddenly, Anna realized that even with what she thought was very good information, she had probably underbid for herself. Sure enough, not much later, she found out that another candidate had been offered $110,000.

PRE-NEGOTIATION/PRE-OFFER FAQ

What *Can* I Talk about Prior to Getting an Offer?

Plenty, of course. You are putting yourself on the market with the goal of getting a job offer. Hence, most of what you will need to talk about is yourself. You may have heard before that job hunting means you are now in sales, and what you are trying to package, market, and sell is yourself. In practice, there are two areas in particular that you will want to highlight as often as possible. The first is selling your competence, your value, and your fit with the company. Again, we leave this part of the content to you and assume you have the skills and the talent for the job.

The second and potentially even more important part is to sell your enthusiasm for the company and for the job. This is part of the general impression management process (refer back to Chapter 2 for more details). Think of the pre-offer conversations as the process of being asked out on a date: nobody wants to ask out someone if they suspect that they might get a "no" in response. Your job during this process is to manage your impression such that you leave no doubt in the minds of the recruiters that you are excited about the possibility of working with them and for them. More times than we can count, we have heard stories from the prime decision-maker in trying to fill a position that the single most important feature that made the top candidate successful in securing the offer was clear enthusiasm for the job. Everyone wants to be wanted, and the more you can convince them that you really want this opportunity, the better your chances of getting that offer for yourself. An awful lot of effort goes into recruiting, and to have the position be refused means that the company has wasted time, money, and emotional energy and still has not solved the problem.

A TRUE STORY

Jenna really wanted the job, and in the end she got it. Later, the manager who hired her admitted to her that even though there were more qualified candidates on their list, she got the offer because she was the one who was the most excited about the job, who followed up with the team after the interview, and who seemed to be the most committed to the whole community serviced by the company.

This does not mean we recommend lying, or even bending the truth, about how likely you are to take the offer if you receive it. We don't suggest that you tell every company that they are your top choice, for instance. Instead, the wisest strategy may be to simply remain positive without committing yourself. After all, your first task is to get the offer. After that, you can evaluate your options, hopefully without burning your bridges or damaging any relationships that you may need in the future. Whatever you do, our advice is to not come across as being ambivalent.

Our recommendation here shouldn't translate merely into general statements like, "I'm so excited about this possibility." Instead, you need to demonstrate your deep interest in the firm, the work itself, the processes used, the product, etc. The candidates who ask detailed questions about the business model, or the creative process, are clearly more interested than those who simply talk about themselves. Again, to return to the dating imagery, you already understand that the date who asks you about your own interests and seems to genuinely care about who you are as a person will come across as more attractive than the self-centered one. The same holds true for job applicants.

TIP

Don't be ambivalent about the job opportunity. Remain enthusiastic about the opportunity throughout the process from the interview through the job negotiation. Demonstrate your interest in the people, the processes, and the target company in general.

What If the Offer Is Delayed?

Time goes by, no job offer is put forth, and their position remains unfilled. This usually indicates that something is going on behind the scenes about which you are unaware. It could be nothing serious. You may have applied for a job that is not critical to their day-to-day operations and everyone is just too busy to make filling this spot rise to the top of the to-do list. But it is also possible that something else is slowing down the process. Perhaps they have an internal candidate in mind, and they are waiting to see if a transfer will work out. Perhaps they are waiting for funding to get approved for a new hire, or for a key internal person to review the candidates before they proceed with any offer. Or, perhaps you are their second or third choice and they are waiting for someone else to either take or reject the offer while they hold you on the line. It may even be the case that they feel that none of the potential candidates were good enough for the job at hand. If you keep the line of communication open with the hiring manager, you can ask to discuss the reasons for the delay and find out what their priorities are. More often than not, people will give you the straight story on what's going on if you just ask for it.

The bottom line is that you cannot force a company to make you an offer of employment. That said, if you find yourself in never-ending talks about employment with no offer being extended (to you or anybody else) and you just cannot take the indecision any longer, then one tactic to consider is using the clock. As with so many tasks, negotiations will often expand to fill the time available. If there is no timeline to make the hire—it can happen this year or next, or even the following year—there may be little expense on their part in delaying the decision, or no incentive to "pull the trigger" and make an offer. The conversation may continue in the relative comfort of the status quo, and just keep talking without any action. To avoid being bogged down by continual talk of potential employment with no action on their part, you *could* give the company a deadline for your availability. We suggest doing this only if you have other offers in hand or are confident other offers will be forthcoming. The risk here is that putting the company under pressure may cause them to walk away. Balance your options here appropriately based on the situation, and read on to understand more about how time pressure works in negotiations.

Can I Use Time Pressure to Speed Up Getting an Offer?

Though we have yet to discuss the ins and outs of negotiating the package itself, the conversation about time pressure applies to both getting offers and negotiating them once they are in hand. Generally speaking, you are better off taking your time when exploring opportunities and negotiating job packages, rather than trying to speed up the process. This is intuitive, and most people feel that allowing the other side to know that they are under time pressure in a negotiation is equivalent to showing that you are desperate and willing to take any deal at all. But in actuality, this need not be the way it works. Research has shown that telling the other side about your time pressure can actually net you *more* out of the deal than will keeping this information to yourself.[4]

By way of example, let's imagine your car has broken down and you need to buy another one today in order to get to work tomorrow. Most people imagine that the right way to handle this scenario is to walk nonchalantly into the car dealer, feign as much indifference as possible about the car to the salesperson, and then negotiate hard with an "I could take this or leave it" attitude. While this strategy may have some value, it overlooks a much more critical component of the exchange, which is the fact that you, as a motivated buyer, are the salesperson's dream come true. Imagine if instead of faking your take-it-or-leave-it attitude, you said, "My car broke down and I will be buying a car today from someone. If I like your deal, it may well be from you. If I don't hear a number I like by 2:00 p.m., I am going elsewhere and someone else will sell me a car today." There are two key points to this story. First, your power is based on whether or not you have alternatives you like—if there were no other car dealers in town, the situation would be quite different. The second point is that time pressure affects all the parties at the table, not just one. So your time pressure is also theirs, and by telling the other side about it, you have now put the burden on them to come up with a deal that you like before you are forced to walk away.

However, the more common situation is one in which the company is putting time pressure on *you* for a quick decision. This taps into another, darker, facet to the psychology of time pressure. This part is critical to understand lest it get in your way accidentally, especially if the company has given you a very short time to decide on their offer (also known as an "exploding offer"). It turns out that the mere *idea* of being under time pressure makes people think, act, behave, and make decisions differently than if they did not believe that there was time pressure. To study this, researchers assigned two groups of people to do the *same* negotiation task in the exact *same* amount of time. In one group, they told the participants that they had plenty of time to complete the task, while in the other group, they were told that their time was limited. Those who felt that their time was squeezed did not think through issues as effectively, were more likely to rely on snap judgments and use stereotypes to reach their conclusions. In addition, they didn't consider as many alternatives before suggesting and agreeing to (suboptimal) deals.[5] Our advice is first to be up front about your timeline with the company, so the company can give their best thinking to presenting offers to you. Second, regardless of whether you feel under time pressure to negotiate with the other side, make sure you keep your composure and take your time to evaluate offers and counteroffers, to help create better options for the deal.

TIP

You will make better decisions if you resist feeling rushed, even in the face of an aggressive deadline.

One last thing that is useful to know about the psychology of time in negotiations: people have a tendency to discount the value of benefits that will be realized later in time than about benefits they can enjoy sooner.[6] In other words, people tend to feel more attracted to issues such as base salary that start immediately than those, such as annual bonuses or profit sharing, that won't pay out for a year's time. Sure, there are good reasons to prefer money in hand as opposed to having to wait for it, but we should rationally decide how much to discount that future payout, and not push it off the table more than is appropriate as a potentially attractive part of a deal.

Hold on There, Did You Just Threaten Me?

Threats rarely occur in the interview or job-negotiation processes very explicitly, but they do occur more subtly, usually in the form of the company referring to another candidate who is both interesting and interested. This mirrors the classic real estate agent's tactic of telling you that there is another serious and motivated buyer about to bid on the property that you are considering. "Act now; the opportunity won't last!" It's true that this lights a fire under one's desire for the object and makes people more willing to concede. Hearing such threats are not pleasant, and they are often designed to push your emotional buttons. How do you deal with such threats? The two most common responses are either to (1) threaten back, perhaps by referring to your own other offers, or (2) panic and reduce your requests so as to seal the deal quickly. Neither instinct is particularly effective. Threatening right back may feel good, satisfying the need for retribution, but that tactic could easily escalate into a messy downward spiral.[7] Lowering the amount that you would accept before being asked to do so is another form of anchoring against your own best interests. Instead, you want to try to diffuse the situation, first by recognizing that a threat has been issued. Even if it is the honest truth that there is another candidate for the position you're pursuing, the fact that you perceive this as a threat means you need to acknowledge and address your likely instincts and then take a step back. Review your goals, and proceed with the conversation in a reasonable manner. Make sure you reiterate how much potential you see in the fit between you and the company and how much value you will add, and then move on as if no (perceived) threat was ever made. No job negotiation will go on forever—you should assume that both of you are trying to tie things up as efficiently as possible.

Can I "Stretch the Truth" about My Worth?

In our experience, the temptation to lie during a job interview or negotiation in an effort to increase the perception of your current market value is strong. Many people feel that "stretching the truth" is just part of the courtship dance and, as such, is fair game as a tactic. We find that deception typically falls into three categories: (1) stating that you have an outside offer that you do not really have, (2) increasing the true value of another offer that you have in hand, or (3) inflating the value of your current salary or employment package. In order to assess the merits of stretching the truth, we need to weigh the potential risks against the potential benefits of being deceptive. The potential benefits are quite straightforward. By artificially inflating your current market value, you may get the hiring company to strive to offer you a better compensation package. In regard to the potential risks, people report them as falling into two main categories: (1) I might get caught, and/or (2) even if I don't get caught, I will not feel right about acting in this way.

The legal definition of fraud says that a statement is fraudulent when the speaker makes a *knowing misrepresentation* of a *material fact* on which the victim reasonably *relies* and which *causes* damage. If you knowingly misrepresent something like your current salary and it causes the other company to overpay you, this qualifies as fraud. To our surprise, when faced with these definitions and explanations, a vocal minority of students often follow up with the question of "Well, how would they ever know?"

On a basic level, it is certainly *possible* for an interviewer to verify information regarding current employment by informally getting this information through a network of colleagues. But on a deeper level, the question itself is troubling. In essence, it is like asking about a "perfect crime" and whether it is okay to act in our own interests, and break the law, merely because we feel confident that we will not get caught. Do you cheat on your taxes because you assume you will not get audited? Would you steal from your company if you felt sure that you found a way to do so without being recognized? Would you shoplift if there were no security system in place to catch you? These examples are direct parallels to the behavior of lying in a job interview simply because you feel sure that you will not get caught. We hope, by highlighting the unequivocal wrongdoing that is involved with this practice, we have encouraged you to think deeply about this practice and be nudged toward the second reason for abstaining from lying, which is the "I wouldn't feel right about doing this" line of logic.

TWO TRUE STORIES

Carly lied when asked what her other offer contained. The company called to confirm with the other company she had mentioned, and found out the truth. She was spared legal action but, needless to say, was not considered by either of those companies again.

On the other hand, Evan lied when the interviewer asked him what he was currently making by inflating the number somewhat, and his lie was not discovered. Yet he says that for the duration of his employment at that job, he never felt right about the situation and felt he had abused his boss's trust from the start. In fact, he said he had trouble looking his boss in the eye. He eventually left the company and was not tempted to lie again.

Since we do not recommend the tactic of lying, our first line of advice is simply to try to make the company highly value you. Then, maximizing your employment package in the job negotiation should be an easier process. A second tool involves offering information about comparable jobs, or market averages, which can also anchor the negotiation in a similar manner as would stretching the truth about your current salary or other offers (see Chapter 4 for a more detailed discussion of this issue, and Chapter 5 for tips on detecting when others are lying to you). These should produce the same anchoring effect without any of the ethical abuse.

SUMMARY

The most important issue at hand here is when to start negotiating and, of equal importance, when not to be negotiating. In summary, you do not want to be forced into negotiating before the right time to do so. *Wait until you get the offer, and get it in writing, before you start negotiating.* Prior to getting that written offer, you should focus on communicating your strengths and your interest in the company and the particular position you are applying for. More specifically:

- Do not accept a verbal offer. Do not negotiate until you have a written offer in your hands.
- Avoid discussing past, current, or future salary prior to getting an offer. Memorize the recommended responses to politely delay the topic if possible.
- Be prepared with alternative information such as comparable offers or the going rate in the industry.
- Don't underestimate the value of your enthusiasm for the job.
- Take time to think, and don't feel pressured to negotiate. Remember that even the idea of time pressure can trip up your best thinking.
- Lying is risky, complicated, and illegal. Rely on your merits instead.

NOTES

1. Stephen, A. T., and M. T. Pham, On feelings as a heuristic for making offers in ultimatum negotiations. *Psychological Science*, 19, 2008: 1051–1058.

2. Galinsky, A., and T. Mussweiler, First offers as anchors: The role of perspective-taking and negotiator focus. *Journal of Personality and Social Psychology*, 81, 2001: 657–669.

3. Shipman, J. W. *The Noel Smith-Wenkle salary negotiation method.* 2010 (cited 2010). Available from http://infohost.nmt.edu/~shipman/org/noel.html.

4. Moore, D. A., Myopic prediction, self-destructive secrecy, and the unexpected benefits of revealing final deadlines in negotiation. *Organizational Behavior and Human Decision Processes*, 94, 2004: 125–139.

5. De Dreu, C. K. W., Time pressure and the closing of the mind. *Organizational Behavior and Human Decision Processes*, 91, 2003: 280–295.

6. Okhuysen, G. A., A. D. Galinsky, and T. A. Uptigrove, Saving the worst for last: The effect of time horizon on the efficiency of negotiating benefits and burdens. *Organizational Behavior and Human Decision Processes*, 91, 2003: 269–279.

7. Malhotra, D., and M. H. Bazerman, *Negotiating genius*. New York: Bantam Dell, 2007.

FOUR

The Actual Negotiation

Once you have a written job offer in hand from the company, it is now your turn to respond, and the negotiation finally begins. Keep in mind that your moment of greatest power comes right after you receive an offer, but before you have accepted it. Prior to getting the offer, the company has expressed interest in you but has not yet committed either logistically or psychologically to the idea that you will be the answer to their needs. But once they have made that commitment, the proverbial ball is in your court, and they are hoping that they can do what it takes to get you to say yes—they *want* you to say yes. This is the time to lay your wishes on the table. In this chapter, we address issues that arise during the actual job negotiation. We discuss how a sense of fairness comes into play for both you and the hiring firm. We also address the tricky topic of trade-offs and concessions of employment terms, and offer suggestions for how to compare competing employment packages effectively. Finally, we end this chapter with some concrete tips and tactics for avoiding the most commonly made mistakes during the actual job negotiation. Note that the related issues of (1) how the negotiation may change in a poor economy and (2) how to negotiate for a promotion or raise when you are already employed will be covered in subsequent chapters (Chapters 8 and 9, respectively).

JUSTIFYING OFFERS AND THE FAIRNESS GAME

It is critically important to justify all of the requests that you put forth in the negotiation. Unless you simply accept a job offer without negotiating, sooner or later you will have to put forth explicit quantifiable numbers. Perhaps the numbers will be regarding salary, bonus, vacation days, profit-sharing plans, or some combination of these. Our advice to you is that this number should *not* be presented in isolation, but instead should come coupled with persuasive logic that feels fair and reasonable to the other side. If your requests adequately address the notion of fairness, you will greatly increase your chances of succeeding.

Research in the field of justice tells us that people care deeply about fairness, sometimes even at the expense of their own best interest.[1] But perceptions of what is "fair" can vary widely. Let's take an example involving three entrepreneurs starting a business, each of whom brings a unique contribution to the table. Maria put in 50 percent of the start-up capital, while Philip and Lisa put in 25 percent each. Philip has significant previous experience in the industry, and Lisa has experience with starting up small companies. Philip has time commitments at home with a spouse and small children, while the other two are single with no children. When it comes time to discuss the division of profits, each relies on a different concept of fairness. Maria says, "I've put in the most money up front so I am absorbing most of the financial risk. Therefore, it's only fair that my potential payout should be highest." This logic is called *equity-based fairness*, and relies on the idea that what you get out of a situation should be commensurate with what you put in. Lisa, on the other hand, says, "We're all in this together and we each bring important and needed aspects to the business. We couldn't do this without all three of our specialized and unique inputs. Therefore we should just split all of our profits with an equal payout to each of us." This logic is called *equality-based fairness*, which is the innate sense of justice you may feel when everyone gets the same amount. Philip, with yet another perspective of what is fair, says the following, "Look, I'm the only one of the three of us with a family to support and I think I should receive a greater share of the payout at least in the early years, because it's more necessary for me and I am taking more of a risk by leaving a steady job with benefits than are either of you." This is a *needs-based fairness* perspective, and is rooted in the idea that resources should go where they are most needed. One of these arguments may resonate with you more than the others, but all three present an articulate and reasonable argument for what is fair. The point illustrated in this example is that each of these approaches to what is fair can have the power to sway people into feeling that a particular solution, or division of rewards, is fair.[2] The critical question for you then becomes which fairness norm is the most effective one for you to make salient in the conversation. Use the fairness norm that is most to your advantage.

As with most situations, in job negotiations it is critically important for both the candidate and the recruiter to feel that the other side has been fair. After all, nobody wants to feel taken advantage of. On a practical level, this is the primary reason that competing offers, market rates, and previous salaries are most commonly used as the benchmark for new salary offers, since these are accepted indicators (by both sides) of what is considered fair. This underscores the importance for you, the candidate, to do extensive research on the market rates for your skills. But our earlier fictional example and the extensive academic literature on fairness also show that there are different ways that you can justify your requests that will appease the recruiter's need for a sense of fairness in what you are asking. Below are examples of how each of these types of logic might work in the job negotiation context.

- "I'm requesting "X" because I am bringing unique skills, experience, and connections with me to your firm"—*equity logic*
- "I'm requesting "Y" because that is what others are making in my same job description in this industry"—*equality logic*
- "I'm requesting "Z" because I need to relocate my whole family and pay off my school loans"—*needs-based logic*

Each approach has its place depending on what is most advantageous to you, and allows the recruiter to feel that what you are presenting is fair and reasonable. This has the potential to raise the level of satisfaction on both sides of the job negotiation, and also increase the chances of the recruiter wanting to accommodate your requests. You can use a combination of reasons, or use different ones at different times. The main point here is that fairness is something that people desire and care very much about, but what makes something feel fair can be "manipulated" and thus can be used in ways that suit your particular situation.

TIP

People on both sides of a job negotiation want a fair and reasonable deal. Strategically create your arguments to support your requests such that they appeal to a sense of fairness. Choose the logic of *equity*, *equality*, and/or *needs* to best present a fairness argument to your advantage.

If you find there are conflicting arguments about what is a "fair" deal, then you may want to verbally acknowledge the company's position. Research has demonstrated that acknowledging the arguments of the other side is a key step toward allowing your own points to be heard. An effective approach is using what's called a "refutational two-sided message,"[3] whereby you not only acknowledge the existence of another point of view, but demonstrate why that particular point is not necessarily valid in this setting, or at least is not as valid as your approach. For example, "I understand that this position has previously paid about $80,000, but the number of positions available for this particular skill set has increased dramatically in the past year, and salaries have risen as a result. Other firms are currently offering six figures for the same type of job." Notice that this argument not only contains elements of fairness based upon both equity and equality, but it also effectively recognizes (and respectfully dismisses) the initial argument.

Be aware that notions about fairness can work against you if you are not careful, especially when you compare your objective outcome with what others have received. This process, referred to as social comparison, is completely normal but can still become problematic for you.[4] Even if you were initially happy with the salary offered to you, you may become notably less happy when you realize you are on the low end of the pay scale relative to what your peers negotiated. We see this happen all the time, even in our classroom exercises. Students who were delighted with the outcomes they negotiated in a particular case and were proud of themselves and their negotiating skills, suddenly become disappointed (and even angry) when they discover that others did better. This resulting sense of angst, and perhaps even embarrassment, can lead to a profound sense of disappointment. While this provides motivation in the classroom for learning, in job negotiations it is not productive. The employment package you attained in a job negotiation, including the salary you received, are the same as they were before you had opportunities for comparison with your peers. Though this might be good information for framing a request for a raise in the future, the immediate truth is that comparisons to others once the negotiation is done can trump logic and make you needlessly unhappy.

For illustrative purposes, let's look at a quiz we use in class.[5]

Your friend is presented with two job offers, and they both expire by the end of this class (i.e., no time for further negotiation).

Job A: The offer from Company 4 is for $85,000 a year. It is widely known that this firm pays all starting MBAs $85,000.

Job B: The offer from Company 9 is for $95,000 a year. It is widely known that this firm is paying some other starting MBAs $105,000.

Students are then asked a few questions about the scenario, including what advice they would give their friend as to which offer to take. Typically, about half of the students recommend their friend take the lower-paying job (A); that is, to take *less* money because the sense of injustice was enough to prompt taking a financial loss in order to protect a sense of fair play. Though there is potentially sound logic in the idea that a company that treats people equally is the better one to work for, we also caution that there may be good reasons for the differences in starting salaries not described in this one sentence. Our advice, all other things aside, is that you should take the offer with more money because your starting salary is one of the best predictors of your future salary, so maximizing it now will reap you benefits for the rest of your career. Put the comparisons out of your head until it's time to ask for a raise.

TIP

Focus on the value of the deal to you, not what others may be getting in their negotiations.

Part of the fairness game is addressed in the way both sides deal with trade-offs and concessions, which is our next topic of discussion.

TRADE-OFFS AND CONCESSIONS

First, let us clarify our terminology when we talk about trade-offs and concessions. A concession is the act of agreeing to a lesser request/amount of something, while a trade-off is a request for more of one thing in exchange for less of something else (hence, the word "trade"). A critical element of the job negotiation is the ability to make trade-offs and to strategically highlight them. On top of the flexibility that trade-offs afford you by way of exchanging components in the deal, it also serves to address yet another element in the fairness game. People like to feel that the other side has been reasonable in conceding some ground from their initial stance, particularly in difficult negotiations where the initial positions are far apart from each other.

Take a very simple negotiation as an example. You are bargaining at a yard sale for a bicycle. The asking price is $100, but you offered to pay

$50, though in fact if push came to shove, you could actually afford the $100. If the seller stuck to his guns and would not budge from the $100 figure, you might still buy the bike, but you would not feel as good about it as you would if the seller had initially asked for $150 and had then come down to $100. This disappointment is partly based on fairness (why should you have to concede your first stance when the seller did not budge at all?) and partly based on the comparison to the initial offer, which placed a psychological anchor (a $100 purchase is better than the $150 asking price, so you are more pleased with it). Either way, people have an innate sense that both sides need to concede something for a "fair" agreement to be reached.

A logical reaction to the bicycle purchase example is that one should create an artificially high counteroffer in a job negotiation with the intent of making a big show about conceding it later (a strategy called "highballing" the negotiation); but this strategy often does not pan out well, as you risk alienating the other side before they even respond. Remember, the overall theme of job negotiations is to remain respectful and reasonable. Instead, the usefulness of this tendency to appreciate concessions made by the other side is more subtle.

While it is true that people in negotiations like to see the other side concede, they also tend to be willing to accept a trade-off rather than just a straightforward concession. For example, you might explain to your potential employer that you would be willing to settle for a lower salary number if extra vacation time were added to the contract (or vice versa). You might be willing to trade a signing bonus or relocation expenses for the opportunity to engage in continuing education classes during the workday. Whatever the trade-offs are, it is important to make clear that you are not just being demanding, but you are actually actively engaged in a give-and-take arrangement within the set of issues that are important to both of you. This fulfills the need for conceding some ground while still keeping focused on what you are trying to obtain with the total employment package.

TIP

Look for and propose trade-offs. Gain items that are important to you by exchanging them for items of lesser importance.

To maximize the power of trade-offs, it is in your best interest to keep as many issues as possible open until the very end of the negotiation. That

is, you don't want to finalize any part of the deal until everything is settled. Oftentimes, our instinct in job negotiations is to move sequentially
from issue to issue, "resolving" each before we move onto the next. No
doubt it is mentally easier and perhaps even more satisfying to go issue
by issue and secure parts of the deal as you go, but to do so closes off
opportunities for trade-offs. Research shows that the more issues you consider simultaneously, the more your final outcome will likely improve due
to finding issues to trade off.[6]

> **TIP**
>
> Keep all issues open until everything is settled and avoid the tempta-
> tion to "lock down" issues in sequence.

Let's now look more specifically at how to figure out the right trade-offs
and concessions for yourself.

USING A TRADE-OFF MATRIX TO ANALYZE WHAT TO TRADE

Job offers typically contain multiple issues, ranging from the basic
salary and benefits to the more company- and person-specific elements
such as annual bonus structure, work-at-home arrangements, etc. To create effective trade-offs between different issues, you first need to be very
clear to yourself about how you value each of the issues. In other words,
you should know how much of one thing you might be willing to give
up in order to get something back on another. This is the "nitty gritty" part
of the job negotiation, and it often feels like comparing apples and oranges
when, ideally, you would like the whole fruit salad, of course. We are
going to present you with a basic framework of a numerical scoring system that you can create for yourself to help you with planning effective
trade-offs. Start with 100 "points" that you can allocate across all of the
different issues up for negotiation. Let's say there are five major things
on the table:

1. Base Salary
2. Annual Bonus Percentage
3. Signing Bonus
4. Vacation Time
5. Flexible Work Arrangements

Next, decide how important each of the five issues is, compared to the others, by allocating an allotment of points to that issue. The more important the issue, the more points you allocate to it. If they are all exactly equal to you, you would give 20 points to each. But, if base salary and flexibility are much more important than the others, you might give those issues 35 points each and leave 10 points for each of the remaining three issues. Let's use that last distribution as a model—35 points toward base salary, 35 points to flexibility, 10 points for annual bonus, 10 for signing bonus, and 10 for vacation time. The next step is to decide what it would take to get the maximum amount of points in each category, and some lesser but still acceptable options below that. Note that true deal-breaker options should not be listed in the chart at all. In other words, determine the range of acceptable values for each issue, and then distribute points to each option. For example, if you have allocated 35 points to the salary issue, and your experience and research shows that salaries tend to range between $105K and $120K, then $120K might get the full 35 points, $115K gets only 30 points, down to $105K for only 20 points. See Table 4.1 for an example of this for each issue.

There are a few things to notice about the values in this table before we proceed to explaining how to use this tool. For one, the fact that two issues are worth more than the others (salary and flexibility) automatically make those the more important things to focus on. But also notice that the point distributions are not uniform—whereas the lowest option for base pay nets 20 points, the lowest option for flex time gets zero. The four options for bonus percentage range uniformly from 10 to 7 points, whereas the four for vacation time jump from 10 to 8 to 3 to 0. It is an entirely personal process to decide what the "right" numbers are for you, but they should accurately reflect your values.

Table 4.1.   Sample Trade-off Matrix

Base Pay	Pts	Bonus %	Pts	Signing Bonus	Pts	Vacation Weeks	Pts	Flex Time	Pts
$120K	35	10	10	$20K	10	5	10	1 day per week	35
$115K	30	8	9	$15K	9	4	8	1 day per 2 weeks	25
$110K	25	6	8	$10K	8	3	3	As needed	10
$105K	20	4	7	$5K	7	2	0	None	0

POINTS TOTAL = (Base Pay Points) + (Bonus % Points) + (Signing Bonus Points) + (Vacation Points) + (Flex Time Points) = _____.

Once you decide on your numerical values, you need to then figure out two other things:

1. What is the total number of points for your best alternative to the job offer in hand? In other words, what will you do if this job offer does *not* work out? If you are currently employed, this may be the value of your current employment package. If you have other offers, this is most likely the value of those (we will return to the discussion of comparing offers in greater detail later within this chapter). Lastly, note that if you are currently unemployed, then this number is zero.

2. What is the *least* total number of points you need to make a deal? Not what you are *hoping* to get, but the lowest number for which, if at the end of the day it was the very best they could do for you, you would take it anyway instead of walking away from the opportunity. This is related to question #1 as you probably do not want anything lower in total value than your viable options. If you are unemployed, you will need to decide on a "lowest acceptable level" without the benefit of a comparable job in hand.

After that, the next step is to play with the numbers and explore different possible scenarios. For example, for the sake of one point, are you really indifferent between an extra $5K in signing bonus and two percentage points in your yearly bonus? If not, this is a good chance to recalibrate and help yourself plan what the better, more equal, substitutions might be. This process can allow you to go into the negotiations armed with more options for how to proceed when negotiations feel stuck and you don't seem to be able to move forward on the issues that are most important to you.

We recognize that quantifying a job negotiation in this way is not always a fun task. But even if you do not end up directly using these numbers in a negotiation, you may find the exercise valuable in other ways. Our students have reported that this focus on comparing issues has allowed them to reframe the negotiation as a give-and-take instead of an all-or-nothing situation. Some students have even come to the startling realization that they did not want the job being offered to them at all, or were about to take a job with a higher salary but a lower total package value than another option. In most cases, doing this quantitative valuation exercise has proved insightful in some manner.

Now that you have some sense of what's important to you, let's take a closer look at how much of this information you should be prepared to reveal during the negotiation.

INFORMATION SHARING

In our years of teaching professionals to negotiate, one of the biggest stumbling blocks is the misdirected belief that people should say as little as possible at the negotiating table. People often seem to feel as if they have been read their Miranda rights and "anything they say can and will be used against them." While it *is* true that some information is better kept to yourself (like your bottom-line salary number—more on this idea in a minute), lots of other information sharing can actually help ease sticking points in the job negotiation. To illustrate this, let's take the fictional example of a negotiation situation in which the husband-and-wife owners of a diner want to sell their restaurant so they can fulfill their lifelong dream of traveling around the world.[7] Because they have already sold their home and bought airline tickets, they feel tremendous pressure to sell to the one restaurant conglomerate who expressed interest in their business. Due to their projected costs associated with the trip, and the need they felt for a nest egg upon their return, the couple had decided that they could not sell the restaurant for less than $750,000. The representative of the restaurant company, however, has been authorized to spend only up to $675,000, since some of the equipment in the kitchen is out of date, and they would need to find ways to staff and train new personnel in that location—particularly an on-site restaurant manager. When negotiating in this situation, many of our students remain focused only on the financial offer-and-counteroffer process without discussing the reasons for the limits each side has set for themselves. After realizing that the company is simply not willing to pay what the couple has decided upon as their bottom offer, many students simply agree to walk away from the negotiations and hope to find another deal instead. But this is a missed opportunity. If both sides were more willing to discuss the particulars of *why* they want what they state as their objectives, new types of agreements can open up. For example, if the restaurant company representative knows about the trip, he or she might be able to offer other goods such as health insurance through their company, or the promise of employment upon return to reduce the couple's needs for a nest egg in hand. If the owners understand the company's concerns over management training, they might be able to offer their services for a limited time to train the new employees before they depart. When money is tight in negotiations (as it so often is), revealing the motivations behind a request can often help break the stalemate by opening the door to new options.

Returning to the context of job negotiations, sharing your rationale can help your future employer defend their decision to accommodate your needs to others inside the firm. If your large signing-bonus request is motivated by the need to get a car in order to commute to work, you might explain that your old car is unreliable and you need to make sure you can get to work every day. If you want a larger year-end bonus to help you pay off your student loans, explain that, and see if the company can cover those costs under their tuition-reimbursement program even if you were not employed there at the time. Even if they cannot help in the end, sharing this kind of logic will make you seem more reasonable and less like you are playing games with them. Bear in mind that your motivations should be reasonable in nature. Wanting a new car with a better sound system will not likely win much support.

TIP

Share as much information as you can about the reasoning behind your requests to allow the firm to help solve your problems. Make your motivations practical and sensible in nature to make it harder for the other side to deny your requests.

There is one more advantage to sharing information in a negotiation, and that is that you are more likely to *get* meaningful information from the other side if you are willing to first *give* some meaningful information away. In psychology, this is called the law of reciprocity, and it is another one of the more reliable human instincts. People have a strong instinct to reciprocate, or to automatically return in kind the behavior that is given to them. If someone is competitive with you, you probably tend to get competitive back. If someone is kind to you, you tend to be kind back. This often works with information in negotiations as well. In a job negotiation, if you share your reasoning for your requests, the other side is more likely to respond with information about the logic behind their offer and, perhaps, the particular constraints they are working under. Such insight may allow you to better understand where the offer has room to move and where it does not, possibly creating new options that neither of you thought to present in the first place, and potentially allowing for an employment arrangement that might not have occurred otherwise.

There is generally only one piece of information you want to guard very cautiously, and that is the *least* amount you would be willing to take in a worst-case scenario. In the negotiation literature, this is called your reservation point, or your walk-away point. For example, let's say you are graduating with your master's degree in accounting, and you really want to work in Miami. You have decided that despite your cohort average salary of $91,200, you won't sign for less than $80,000, but would take that amount if you needed to. If a potential employer is interested and you tell them that you would not accept less than $80,000 as a bottom line, you are essentially saying, "Offer me $82,000 and I will have to say yes (or look foolish if I say no)." If those employers walked in prepared to offer $91,000, in all likelihood they no longer will!

Job negotiations are not always clear cut, and so of course there are times when you probably do want to reveal your reservation point. The rule of thumb is that your bottom-line package should be kept under wraps *unless* it seems the company is not meeting your lowest acceptable possible deal, but you would still like the chance to work there. Returning to the example where your walk-away point in a particular job negotiation was $80,000 on the salary issue, let's say that although you had initially asked for $85,000, they have remained steadfast at $75,000. In this case, if that job is really the one you want but only at $80,000 (and not below), you might want to tell them so before walking away. You might say something along the lines of, "I'm really interested in this job and working at your firm, but I can't make it happen for less than $80,000. Below $80,000, I'll need to decline. If you can possibly meet me at that number, we can have a deal." Again, this information only makes sense at the *end* of a negotiation when you have already exhausted the possibility of getting more, not at the beginning when you still do not know what might be possible. It is a "last resort" tactic to use only before declining the offer.

TIP

Don't reveal your walk-away point, unless as a last resort before actually walking away.

COMPARING MULTIPLE OFFERS: USING THE OFFER RATING SYSTEM

If you are fortunate enough to have multiple job offers in hand, you will want to compare them to each other. Because the offers most likely contain multiple issues, this can be a tricky process. Hence, we now introduce a second scoring system that is particularly well suited for comparing multiple job offers. This system works best if you already have written job offers in hand, but even without that, you can usually imagine different scenarios to try out just to give yourself a sense of how different combinations of things might stack up. Note that this is different from the Trade-off Matrix we introduced earlier. The Offer Rating System relies on *actual data* about different job packages. The Trade-off Matrix is instead a tool only for quantifying your *own* preferences so that you would be prepared to offer the most effective trade-offs in the actual job negotiation.

Let's say that you are comparing job offers from three different firms. The first step in the Offer Rating System is to identify all of the aspects of the employment package, or at least the four to five most important ones. For simplicity's sake, let's use four issues here: money, opportunity for growth, stability, and location/commuting time. Once you have identified the main issues, weight them according to your priorities by dividing 100 percent into smaller components for each issue. In our example we weight salary the most at 50 percent, growth opportunity and stability are equally important at 20 percent apiece, and the commute is lowest at 10 percent. Table 4.2 shows what our Rating Offers System table looks like so far.

Next, you can start filling in the chart (ignoring for the moment the weights you just assigned to each of your top four issues) by rating each job offer on each of the areas of interest. For example, you can force each column to have a best, middle, and worst by only using numbers 1, 5, and 10, or you can decide to give each job any number from 1 to 10 to give yourself more freedom to adequately reflect the magnitude of the differences between some of the jobs. More specifically, if one job offered you $100K, one $90K, and another $80K, you might want to give them 10, 9, and 8 points, respectively. Or, you might want to give them 10, 8, and 4 points, respectively, to indicate that $80K is below a reasonable threshold for you on that issue. Either way, once you have scored each job on each issue, the next step is to then multiply the number ratings by the percentage weight-factor you assigned earlier and then add across. You can see, numerically, which job "wins" and why by engaging in this

Table 4.2. Blank Sample Offer Rating System

	Interest #1: Money	Interest #2: Opportunity for Growth	Interest #3: Stability	Interest #4: Location/ Commute	Total
Weight	50%	20%	20%	10%	
Job 1					
Job 2					
Job 3					

Table 4.3. Complete Sample Offer Rating System

	Interest #1: Money	Interest #2: Opportunity for Growth	Interest #3: Stability	Interest #4: Location/ Commute	Total
Weight	**50%**	**20%**	**20%**	**10%**	
Job 1	8	10	3	2	**6.8***
Job 2	2	7	7	10	**4.8**
Job 3	6	5	9	8	**5.8**

* $[(8 \times 50\%) + (10 \times 20\%) + (3 \times 20\%) + (2 \times 10\%)] = 6.8$

activity. Table 4.3 displays what our example (using a full 1–10 rating system) might now look like.

As with the Trade-off Matrix, we often find that people are initially reluctant to do this quantitative exercise, but almost everyone appreciates it after the fact. Many times, it reinforces implicit beliefs that were not initially quantifiable. Other times, people are surprised when the "wrong" company unexpectedly wins out. When this happens, what have you learned? Hopefully you have gained some new insights about yourself and the fact that your weights were "wrong" originally in the sense that they were not true to what you hope to achieve in the negotiation. In other words, what you wrote on paper in terms of your priorities did not gel with your gut feelings about what you actually hope to do with your time.

For example, Job #1 above "won," with Job #3 in second place and Job #2 in third place. Let's say you tabulated these results and realized with a sinking heart that according to this chart, you were going to have to take Job #1 when the thought of commuting an hour each way in traffic just makes your skin crawl. After doing this exercise, you suddenly become aware that you do not care that much about the higher salary if it would cost that much of your time and sanity. This realization would be good evidence for you that you had underweighted the location/commute variable in this chart, and should reassign the weights until it both looked right objectively on paper and felt right when a particular decision is indicated. By quantifying the issues and interests, the Offer Rating System allows you to explore this kind of faulty logic and reconcile yourself to what it is you want and need out of a job in addition to objectively ranking job offer desirability.

This table can also allow you to understand where a particular offer is falling short of others. In the above example, you might want to return to Job #2 and explain to them that there are many attractive features of their firm and offer, but the money is out of line with other offers. Though ideally money is not the most important reason for choosing what you do with your time, it is always a variable in job offer situations. You can respectfully request that to make your decision based on the more relevant aspects of skills, career growth, and fit with the firm, you would like them to make the money element more consistent with other offers or market rates. Keep in mind that although blatant self-interest is unattractive to recruiters, this approach feels reasonable and fair, and definitely does not reek of a candidate who is trying to create a bidding war or milk the offer for whatever can be obtained.

TIP

Use the following language with the company you actually want to work for, when a higher competing offer/market value comes from less desirable jobs. "I have an offer in hand for X. I'd like to ask whether you might be able to make the money elements (or whatever the issue on the table is) more similar so I can take money out of the equation when I make my decision and really choose the job that is the best fit."

USING OTHER OFFERS AS A SPRINGBOARD

Talking about other offers can fall into either the category of "other offers you have" (which is relatively intuitive) or the category of "other offers you don't have" (which is less obvious, and can also be described as comparable jobs or market trends). Just like talking about your current salary, referring to other offers that you already have in hand is more helpful if it happens to be a strong and attractive offer (though even a weak one can be a positive signal of your desirability on the market). Oftentimes, however, you don't have the luxury of referring to a strong current salary or other offer. In fact, most often, that is why you are looking for job offers in the first place! Instead, sometimes it can be just as effective to talk about comparable offers and jobs *even if you do not have them in hand yourself.* This is not to suggest that we advocate lying or stretching the truth by stating or even implying that you have received an offer that you have not. While this might be potentially tempting, it constitutes a fraudulent act. Instead, being wholly upfront by telling the company what your understanding of offers for similar positions *would* look like can often be enough to anchor the conversation in the place where you want it. This can be knowledge you gain directly from other companies, from colleagues working in the industry, or from headhunters. The more specific the information, the better, but any information you have will help you in this part of the process.

A TRUE STORY

Sarah, a scientist, was interviewing for jobs. But, as is all too common, the interview schedules for the two companies she was most interested in did not line up perfectly. Company A needed her response to their offer by December 15, since they would lose their line of funding on January 1 and needed time to make an offer to their second choice if she turned them down. Company B interviewed her on December 7, but their other top candidate for the position was unavailable to interview until after January 3, so their decision would not come until mid-January. While at the interview with Company B, Sarah asked the recruiter there, "Would you mind telling me what the offer would look like if I *were* to receive it?" and then got the details of the package. Upon her next conversation with Company A, she told them that while she did not have an offer in hand from Company B, she was informed what their package would look like, and it was stronger in two areas. Company A agreed to match the offer in one of the places and make up some of the difference in the other.

In the example above, using another (potential) offer as an anchor can also help signal which aspects of a deal are more important to you. With or without the advantage of holding another written offer in hand, by saying "Other jobs [be as specific here as possible about what jobs you are referring to] are offering better terms with respect to both administrative support and budgets for conference travel. I don't feel the need to ask for extra administrative support since I think I can accomplish my work successfully with what you offer, but I do think the extra travel and conference budget would be quite helpful," you have indicated that even though they have not offered you more administrative support, you *have already made a concession* by not requesting it.

TIP

Use market rates to signal concessions, and as the basis for your (reasonable) requests.

CONTINGENCY COUNTEROFFERS

A contingent contract is a bet on some future outcome. In the case of job negotiations, it usually refers to some sort of early review or chance for promotion once you have had a chance to prove yourself. Negotiating for an early promotion review or raise is a classic example of this.

A TRUE STORY

Marianne, a PhD graduate, was being hired by a consulting firm at a level below that for which she felt capable. But, since the firm typically hired MBA students, they were not sure of her fit. To make this deal work for all parties, they agreed to review her performance in 6 months instead of the standard 12 months and then promote her early if she was indeed capable of advancing to the next level.

One note of caution is that with contingent deals such as these, it is even more important to make sure that the details are established in writing, since this kind of arrangement can often slip under the radar if it is not explicitly clarified in detail. Contingent contracts need not be limited to job titles and rates of pay, but can also cover work arrangements such as flextime, job sharing, and responsibilities, as the following example illustrates.[8]

A TRUE STORY

Elise was negotiating for a job that required a five-day-a-week presence, when she preferred to be in the office only three days a week and to work from home for the other two (as the job was quite far from her home, and relocating her family was not an option for her). The company decided to pass on her, since the five-day-a-week element was not negotiable to them, though they really wanted her. Instead of accepting this and moving on, Elise decided to give it one more shot. She drafted a letter to the head of the department she hoped to work for, and copied the CEO of the company. In it, she told them how much she wanted this job and how much of an asset she believed she would be for the department as well, regardless of a three-day-per-week presence in the office. She had given some thought to how she could add value to the group when she was not present, and realized that she was equipped to build a much-needed web presence for them from home. In her letter she said, "I believe that within a year's time, you will be as happy with me and my work with the three-days-in and two-days-out arrangement as you would have been from someone in the office all five days a week. I'm confident enough of this to propose the following deal:

- Pay me 25 percent less than what you originally offered me.
- Take the extra money, and put it in escrow for the year.
- If, at the end of the year, you are happy with my performance, back-pay me the extra money, and consider me for a promotion at that point.
- If you are unhappy with the arrangement for any reason, I will leave at the end of the year and the department can have the extra funds for their own use.

The company was so impressed with (1) her inspired thinking, and (2) her commitment to the opportunity, that they gave her the job, but refused her suggestion to pay her less than what they had offered. Needless to say, they were thrilled with her work.

Though contingent-based employment packages are more the exception than the norm, we have seen these types of contingent counteroffers work successfully enough to warrant bringing it to your attention. When it works, both parties walk away even more satisfied with the arrangement.

THE TOP 10 *DON'TS*: COMMON MISTAKES AND HOW TO AVOID THEM

Thus far, we have discussed how to proceed in a job negotiation. Equally important are the ways people often get waylaid. Here is our list of the top 10 mistakes people often make in the actual job negotiation and suggestions for sidestepping them.

1. *Accepting a job offer immediately upon its offering*. Don't respond immediately to any offer given, even if it delights you. Take the time to seriously consider it—this serves you well in three different ways:

    a. First, it gives you the opportunity to think through whether there are any elements you would like to follow up with, or any further requests you might want to make, and also to compare it to any other offers without the pressure of the in-the-moment conversation. Everyone thinks more clearly when they are not in the middle of this emotion-laden discussion.

    b. Second, taking time to consider the offer will make them feel that their offer was about right and that they did not seriously overbid for you. The "Winner's Curse" describes the way people tend to feel worse about their outcomes when they know the other side feels great about theirs.[9] Accepting too quickly in any negotiation can lead the other side to think they have overpaid. For example, a colleague bought a used car from a friend. The seller was asking $4,500, and the buyer said "How about $4,000?" The seller accepted, and the buyer later reported that he would actually have felt better about the purchase if the seller had countered with $4,200! Time delays between offer and acceptance have been shown to increase satisfaction in the deal.[10]

    c. Lastly, it gives the other side a positive impression of your ability to keep a level head and consider information fully without rushing to judgment.

2. *Asking if the job offer is negotiable. Don't* ask if an offer is negotiable; just jump right in and put your requests on the table.[11] If you ask a global question like that and get a "no" as a response, there's nothing left to discuss without making yourself look bad. If you focus the conversation instead on specific issues, you may actually discover an area where they may have some flexibility.

3. *Being halfhearted.* Don't let the stress of the situation prompt you to make a "half-request." This is when you bring up something that you would like to request, but do it in a meek and almost apologetic way, signaling from the get-go that you do not really expect the other side to acquiesce nor will you be offended if they do not accept the counteroffer. As long as you are respectful and reasonable in your negotiation, you don't need to be apologetic or halfhearted.

4. *Giving in just to be polite.* Don't negotiate against yourself. Wait out silences, and let the other side respond to your requests. Even in classroom mock negotiations with no real consequences, we have seen students suggest something, take the ensuing silence as a sign that the other side is displeased with the offer, and immediately jump in and suggest a second, more "palatable" amount. In

negotiations terminology, we call this a unilateral concession; in common sense, we call it a mistake.

5. *Offering a range of numbers that would be acceptable to you.* When stating a number, don't give a range, but instead stick to a single value. Ranges only confuse the conversation.

6. *Focusing exclusively on your salary.* Don't focus exclusively on the salary number. Remember instead to consider the value of the total compensation package. Though salary is very important, don't forget that it may be a sticking point for the company for internal reasons of equity or funding, and that they may have more flexibility in other areas instead that still add value for you overall.

7. *Not asking for what you want.* Don't be afraid to make a request just because you might be denied. As long as you haven't offended anyone, you can still take the original offer as it was stated if necessary.

8. *Expecting concessions from your future employer.* Don't get caught up in getting concessions just for the sake of getting concessions. Stay focused on what is of most critical importance to you. Some companies really don't have any room to move from what they offered you first, and it might be reasonable even without adjustment.

9. *Accepting the "job" in concept without any specific details.* Don't lose track of the details in each and every conversation. Finalize details beyond the obvious: reporting structure, job description, evaluation processes, promotion timeline, and the like can be useful tools to have set on paper once the job begins.

10. *Not closing the deal.* Stop negotiating when either (or both) of two things happens:
    a. The other side seems annoyed with the continuation of the process.
    b. When the back-and-forth is over something small. Nobody cares that much about the last $1,000, but at that point everyone judges the person doing the asking.

SUMMARY

Here are the top five things to remember regarding the actual job negotiation:

- You have the most power right after the initial offer is made. Use it to your advantage by taking time to think. Stay focused on the issues that you have prioritized.

- Fairness matters—to you and to the employer:
  - Focus on the package that works for you, and not what you think other people are getting.
  - Justify your requests by applying the principles of equity-based, equality-based and/or needs-based fairness.
- Although your starting salary is one of the best predictors of your future earnings, both at this company and at others, there are lots of other issues on the table in job negotiations, and they may have more room for movement.
- Share information! If you are making trade-offs, let the employer know. Give your reasons for requesting certain items. It will work in your favor and help the employer to help you meet your needs.
- Use the rating systems provided, or create your own, to aid in evaluating issues and offers. Identify quantitatively exactly how much value each issue on the table has for you.

NOTES

1. Pillutla, M. M., and J. K. Murnighan, Unfairness, anger, and spite: Emotional rejections of ultimatum offers. *Organizational Behavior and Human Decision Processes*, 68, 1996: 208–224.

2. Schwinger, T., Just allocation of goods: Decisions among three principles. In *Justice and social interaction: Experimental and theoretical contributions from psychological research*, G. Mikula, Editor. New York: Springer-Verlag, 1980.

3. Dillard, J. P., and L. J. Marshall, Persuasion as a social skill. In *Handbook of Communication and Social Interaction Skills*, J. O. Green and B. R. Burleson, Editors, 479–513. Malwah, NJ: Lawrence Erlbaum, 2003.

4. Adams, J. S., Inequity in social exchange. In *Advances in experimental psychology*, L. Berkowitz, Editor, 267–299. New York: Academic Press, 1965.

5. Bazerman, M. H., G. Loewenstein, and S. White, Reversals of preference in allocating decisions: Judging an alternative versus choosing among alternatives. *Administrative Science Quarterly*, 37, 1992: 220–240.

6. Weingart, L. R., R. J. Bennett, and J. M. Brett, The impact of consideration of issues and motivational orientation on group negotiation process and outcome. *Journal of Applied Psychology*, 78, 1993: 504–517.

7. Goldberg, S. B., *Texoil*. Evanston, IL: Dispute Resolution Research Center, Kellogg School of Management, 1997.

8. Amoroso, L., Contingent contracts and job negotiations. Working Paper. Chicago, IL: Roosevelt University, 2009.

9. Bazerman, M. H. and W. F. Samuelson, I won the auction but don't want the prize. *Journal of Conflict Resolution*, 27, 1983: 618–624.

10. Srivastava, J., and Oza, S., Effect of response time on perceptions of bargaining outcomes. *Journal of Consumer Research*, 33, 2006: 266–272.

11. Cates, K., Tips for negotiating a job offer. Unpublished manuscript. Evanston, IL: Kellogg School of Management, Northwestern University, 1997.

FIVE

Powerful Communication

Communicating well in a job negotiation, as in any professional setting, is often difficult. In this chapter, we give an overview of some commonly experienced challenges and ways to overcome them. Then we focus specifically on the type of power dynamic most people encounter during a job negotiation, when it feels like the potential employer has more authority and higher status than you do during the conversation. We talk about politeness (how much is the right amount, and what types get in the way of getting your message across), and about what types of communication signal dominance versus submission. Finally, we cover listening skills as part of this chapter, because although we all listen as a natural part of our daily interactions, most people unfortunately do this poorly much of the time.

Communicating gets easier and more efficient the longer you have known the other person. You can take shortcuts in your speech when you have a shared history. For example, a manager might say to a colleague something that seems to be in "code," such as "there it goes again," where both parties understand perfectly what the "it" means but nobody from the outside could possibly decode the statement. Similarly, people are better at persuading others whom they have known over time, because they can adjust their tactics as they get feedback on what works and what does not.[1] Unfortunately, conversations in a job negotiation context are typically at the other end of the spectrum and involve someone with whom you are not well acquainted.

Conversations with strangers contain an inherent tension between remaining polite and respectful while still spelling out exactly what you are trying to say without ambiguity. Fortunately, there are other common-alities besides past experience that you might share with the potential employer (or the person you are negotiating with) to aid your communica-tion. Any degree of shared cultural and/or personal background can make for more effective communication. Finding the commonalities between yourself and the other party can help the job negotiation process not just by building trust, but also through more effective communication. How-ever, in this chapter, we are going to assume the worst-case scenario whereby the person facing you in the job negotiation is someone without any of the natural advantages of easily identified similarities, and we will talk about tools for effective communication even in this difficult setting.

THE CURSE OF KNOWLEDGE: DO YOU REALLY UNDERSTAND WHAT I'M SAYING?

One of the biggest pitfalls identified by the communication research lit-erature is something known as the curse of knowledge. This ominous-sounding title refers to our basic overestimation of the knowledge base and understanding of the other side.[2] For example, if you are talking about your previous job, you are likely to explain things in a way that uninten-tionally assumes that the listener understands a great many of the details about that job. While some listeners may well understand it all, the com-munication literature suggests that most people assume too much from their audience. In reality, the other side really does not catch as much of what you are trying to tell them as you thought they would. In order to avoid "talking down" to people, we have a tendency to instead talk over their heads. On the listening side, people also have a strong reluctance to say, "I have no idea what you're talking about," or even hint at this unflat-tering truth. Instead, as educated professionals, we tend to cover up our knowledge gaps instead of publicly acknowledging them. Have you ever nodded and said "Uh huh" to things about which you actually had little to no understanding? If so, you're in good company. We all tend to do this to some extent, and doing so compounds the effects of the curse of knowl-edge by leading others to think they are effectively communicating with us when in fact they are not.

Sometimes people even use this concept on purpose. By telling you far more than you could ever understand about a topic, a person hopes to sound very high-level and impressive, and thus persuade you. This tactic, called a snow job (or data dump) relies on your basic reluctance to admit that you are in over your head in the conversation. Software salespeople, for example, may do this by overloading you with discussions of specs and features that you don't really need, in order to make the product (and themselves) look all the more impressive. Instead, remember that there is actually power in the ability to respect yourself as a competent professional and say, "I'm not familiar with that; can you tell me more about it?"

Returning to the context of job negotiations, the curse of knowledge is a pitfall that you can easily avoid by asking questions as you present information to make sure you are being well understood. Questions like, "Have you worked with that system before?" or "Are you familiar with this process?" help you to assess how much detail to give. The rule of thumb, though, is that it's better to over-explain than to under-explain. In addition to technical work details, this principle holds true when you are explaining your position or justifying your requests in a job negotiation. Your explanation can go a long way toward convincing the other side of the merit of your requests. To be fully understood, your rationale needs to be communicated well.

> **TIP**
>
> Don't assume the recruiter knows what you are talking about. Explain things in clear and detailed ways. Ask clarifying questions if you yourself don't understand something that's been said.

CIALDINI'S PSYCHOLOGY OF PERSUASION

Of course you know from experience that getting others to agree to the things you want them to do is no easy feat, and the way you frame your requests can have a significant impact on the likelihood of successful persuasion. People judge others based on what persuasion tactics they use and tend to dislike the feeling of being persuaded. The key to all persuasion is to make sure that you are comfortable with what you say and that you yourself would not feel "put upon" if someone said the same things to you. This section outlines the psychology behind persuasion and may be directly useful for you—or, conversely, you may not feel comfortable and respectful using these tools in your job negotiation. In any case, see if you find any tips that might be helpful for you and your particular situation (whether it is a job interview, a job negotiation, or both).

Robert Cialdini, a social psychologist in Arizona, has done a lifetime of work in the area of the psychology of persuasion, and has summarized the entire field into six key principles that apply to human psychology across the board.[3] Below, we will explain each one of his concepts and then discuss how they relate to the job negotiation. In no particular order, they are:

1. Scarcity
2. Authority
3. Liking
4. Social Proof
5. Commitment and Consistency
6. Reciprocation

Scarcity

This is the idea that if something is perceived to be rare or hard to find in any way, then it must be valuable. There are numerous examples of this in our daily lives. Marketing campaigns announce that "there's nothing else like our product" to show how rare it is. Supermarkets declare a particular item restricted to "two per customer" to demonstrate that availability is limited. Even the classic advertising gimmick, "Act now, this deal won't last long!" plays on our desire to seize a rare opportunity. The idea that we can have something that is not readily available to everyone else, nor perhaps even available to us at a later time, is powerful. Why does this work on us? It relates to psychological reactance,[4] which is sometimes referred to as reverse psychology. Human beings of all ages have an innate instinct to want what they cannot have. This can be seen when two-year-olds throw fits when told that they cannot have something, through the teenage years when defiance is second nature, and straight into adulthood.

For you as a job candidate, the recommended strategic task then is differentiation. Making yourself stand out as unique and a one-of-a-kind opportunity for the company can ignite this type of "must-have-it" response. You do not want to overplay it, but you do want to make sure you highlight ways that your skills, experience, and abilities are different from other candidates that the firm may be considering. A second, potentially more *risky* tactic that is related to the principle of scarcity is using deadlines to your advantage. Your own, softer, and more respectful version of the "Act Now!" logic might run something like this: "I'm very interested in this position, but I feel I should tell you that I will need to make my final decision in the coming weeks about where my career will go next. At that time, I will either move to a new position or get immersed in a big project at my current job. Then I would not be willing to leave again for some time." Of course, if you have a competing offer in hand, that is an even easier way to present this kind of strategic framing. (If you are willing to wait longer for the chance at this particular job opportunity, though, you probably don't want to try this.)

TIP

Accentuate your uniqueness by explicitly highlighting (i.e., selling) your differences from other candidates.

Authority

Just as the term implies, this principle describes how people are hardwired to respect and defer to those who hold a position of authority. The twist is that any kind of authority influences us, not just actual positions of power. Even the appearance of authority can be powerful, so dressing the part for the job you want (including not just your clothing but also your portfolio, the pen you carry, etc.) is important. Similarly, being able to claim a title of any kind beside your name signals your authority in a very straightforward way. Finally, of course, being able to demonstrate or suggest that you are an expert in any domain is also a pathway to authority. Again, while you don't want to be self-aggrandizing, neither do you want to downplay your accomplishments and your degrees.

TIP

Dress the part, showcase your knowledge, and if you have advanced degrees or certificates of training of any kind, list them after your name prominently on your correspondence.

Liking

We have spoken before about the power of similarity in getting others to like you. There are also other routes to this outcome. One powerful route to being liked is by association. Have you ever heard the phrase, "Kill the messenger"? In that case, when people are associated with negative events and outcomes, you may feel less inclined to want to associate with them. On the flip side, when people are associated with good events and outcomes, you may think more positively of them (even if objectively, the two are unrelated). There are numerous real examples of each of these phenomena. Hate mail sent to weather reporters in response to terrible weather, cars rated as faster and better designed when the picture of the car contained a beautiful model standing near it, and products being sold at greater rates when associated with the Olympic Games all work on this very principle.[5] People even respond more positively to ideas presented while they are eating good food![6] It is also assumed that we have similar characteristics as our friends. How can this work for you in a job negotiation situation? This is the time to encourage yourself to name-drop: successful people that you are connected with as well as successful businesses or successful situations that you have been a part of can all lend their cache to you. You will have to judge how and when to speak about this kind of information, since you don't want it to appear calculated, but they are persuasive points to get on the table.

Another shortcut to liking is through compliments. According to Cialdini, people are highly predictable suckers for flattery. Of course, egregious ingratiation can be annoying, but it is surprising how much it takes to cross that line. Impressively for your role as a job candidate, it turns out that *flattery works on people even if they know you have something to gain from flattering them.* Though this is not recommended as a tactic to use, flattery even seems to work when the content is blatantly untrue! Consider the car salesman who repeatedly mailed cards to his target customers saying merely, "I like you," and saw incredible sales as a result.[7] If you are at all uncertain about trying to flatter the interviewer directly, stay on more comfortable ground and praise the heck out of the company. This has essentially the same effect, because you are implying that the recruiter has made a good choice in being a part of this organization. And, based on the principles of association, it is also pleasing to the recruiter to be thought of as a part of such a great place. Be genuine, but make sure you say out loud all of the positive thoughts you can muster about this particular situation. Compliments to their group, their organization, or their accomplishments will go a long way.

TIP

Present yourself as associated with positive outcomes and successful people whenever possible. Practice comments designed to politely flatter.

Social Proof

Social proof is the age-old rule of thumb that "if everyone else is doing it, then it must be a good idea." People feel naturally inclined to engage in all sorts of behaviors—from donating, to being helpful, to making purchases—if they feel that others (especially others who are similar to them) have done so in the past. This is particularly powerful in situations of uncertainty, meaning that there are doubts as to what is the appropriate course of action. Hiring situations are often nothing if not uncertain; here sits a hiring manager, sifting through resume after resume of complete strangers, trying to discern which traits and characteristics will best predict a good fit for the company both professionally and personally. No wonder it makes such a difference to have someone inside the company hand over your resume and vouch for your quality! That's one form of social proof at work. Another is one that may be out of your control: other employment and/or other offers. We have heard this called the "dusty coal" process, whereby a job candidate sits in a barrel as a dusty piece of coal until one potential employer picks it up, dusts it off, and sees the diamond underneath. In one employer's hand, the coal now sparkles like a diamond to everyone else. Suddenly, everybody wants a chance to hire this individual who, mere moments ago, was desperate for any attention at all from recruiters. This is also why it is so much more powerful to look for a job while you still have one than from a position of unemployment. You seem much more employable when someone else has already invested their money in employing and training you. This is social proof at work.

> **TIP**
>
> Work to gather interest in your candidacy from a few sources, either internal or external to the organization you are negotiating with. In addition, without gloating or threatening, do not hide the fact if other companies are interested in you as well.

Consistency and Commitment

Simply put, it creates uncomfortable internal angst to go back on your word, your decisions, or even your pattern of behaviors. This is why store salespeople for large purchases (mattresses, even cars) often pressure you for a "fully refundable," small down payment immediately, knowing that once you have committed to part of the sale, it becomes very unlikely that you will go back on your decision. Even telemarketers who call and start by asking you how you are today are not merely being polite but are activating your side of the conversation, one that you will hopefully follow up with agreement to purchase something later on in the call. Similarly being asked to comply with small requests (and agreeing) seems to be a gateway to getting compliance on larger requests.

In the job situation, this approach can work in your favor if you have the opportunity to ask questions of the recruiter and frame your conversation around your suitability as an employee there. Fundamentally, you want to ask, "Do you feel that I would be able to contribute value to your organization?" though you might need to be a little softer in your approach. Questions about the specifics of the job might be a good entrée, to be followed up with questions about whether they feel that your particular skills or experiences would be useful in helping to accomplish those activities and/or goals. If you get affirmative responses, the principle of consistency and commitment would predict that you are more than halfway home in leading the recruiter to respect his or her earlier assertions on your value to the company.

> **TIP**
>
> If possible, have the recruiter acknowledge that your particular skills and experiences would benefit the company.

Reciprocity

Last but certainly not least comes reciprocity, which is the inclination to return favors and remove yourself from perceived indebtedness. This affects many aspects of daily life, from the more direct example of giving gifts to those who have gifted you to the more obscure example of the pressure you may feel (consciously or not) to purchase something or donate money after you have been given something for "free." While it's unlikely that you will be able to bestow a favor or give something of value to the recruiter in a job negotiation, there are other forms that the principle of reciprocity can take, which might be more helpful for this context. The first is the giving of concessions. When negotiating, people have a natural sense that they should all try to concede about the same amount and "meet in the middle" of their initial demands. Offering concessions is one way to activate the principle of reciprocity and put pressure on the other side to come up with a concession of similar magnitude.

A TRUE STORY

Sam was offered a position at a medium-sized firm, and it was his top choice even though the offered salary was well below what he was currently making (and even on the low side of industry norms). However, the company wanted him to spend about three weeks overseas setting up a quality control program at a manufacturing site. This was not attractive to Sam since he would have to leave his wife and small children at home, and three weeks felt like too long an absence from his family. Sam made it clear during the negotiation that this was not something he wanted to do for family reasons, but that he wanted the deal to work and he wanted to help the company out in any way he could, so he was willing to make the trip. The company, in turn, responded by sending him a revised employment contract to sign that included, much to his surprise, a new salary number that matched his previous wages.

Sometimes people are tempted to ask for something that they actually *don't* want, to then make a big deal about conceding it and thus put the onus on the other side to grant your second, much more reasonable, request. The tactic is called a bogey and is generally ill advised in our opinion: What if the other side gives you what you did not want? What if they just write you off as being unreasonable? If the other side balks at your request in any way, at best you may get the opportunity to backpedal and say something like "Oh, I can actually change my request to X . . ." and lose a lot of credibility in the process. Instead, as discussed in more detail in Chapter 4, you can contrast what you are currently requesting against something else that you could have, but have declined to, request. This implies that you have already made a concession, and the other side should, according to the principle of reciprocity, want to do the same for you.

A TRUE STORY

Amelia told her recruiter about a few wishes that she would *not* be requesting. She said, "Ideally, I had hoped for a schedule that would accommodate two work-from-home days a week in order to minimize the time lost with commuting and maximize the time I could dedicate for my projects. I understand, however, that you value face time, so I'm only requesting that one day a week be included in my contract." He gave her the one-day flex as requested, and slightly increased her vacation time as well.

TIP

Share your thoughts on what your ideal (pie-in-the-sky) package would look like, and then share which areas you are prepared to concede in order to start a chain of reciprocal concessions.

POWERFUL VERSUS POWERLESS: COMMUNICATING UP

Even if you have other attractive job options, most recipients of a job offer feel that the recruiter is the one who holds more power in the conversation. The recruiter typically has higher status in the organization and certainly has the power to influence the hiring decision. As a job candidate, this sense of lacking power activates certain patterns of speech that can sometimes muddy the waters of communication and lead to less effective requests in job negotiations. This section delves into the notion of communicating effectively when there are perceived differences in power.

Believe it or not, there's a whole school of academic research on a topic termed politeness theory, which basically defines politeness as the act of trying to make sure nobody loses face in the conversation.[8] Not surprisingly, it turns out that people in positions of lower status spend more time trying to make sure they do not offend their higher-status counterpart. Here is a shortcut to figuring out who has higher status in any conversation between two people you do not know: look to see who is allowed to interrupt the other speaker. We have unwritten rules that we all understand about what is polite and what is not, and one of them is that if people outrank you, you let them speak over you, but you yourself do not cut them off. But politeness can also be a trap that prevents you from communicating effectively.

One of the ways that low-power people tend to distort their speech in order to make sure it does not sound too bold or aggressive is by performing what is known as indirect speech acts. These indirect speech acts are subtle, but important. As you know, we have command over thousands and thousands of words in our working vocabularies, and we can combine them in countless ways to express our thoughts. In fact, we rarely use the same sentences twice. Even when we are just trying to repeat what someone else has told us, we catch the meaning and unintentionally construct different sentences, using different words, to express ourselves. However, not all choices for sentences are equally clear and unambiguous in their meaning, and this is where we get to indirect speech acts. For example, let's say that Carol wanted to make a request to her spouse to wash the dishes in the sink. The most direct possible sentence is the command version, "Wash the dishes!" But that may not feel polite to her, so she might add polite qualifiers and change the command to a question: "Can you wash the dishes please?" Though different, it is still pretty clear what she is asking for. Now consider those two examples in the context of similar sentences, all designed with the same goal in mind:[9]

1. Wash the dishes!
2. Can you wash the dishes, please?
3. Would you mind awfully if I asked you to wash the dishes?
4. It might help to wash the dishes.
5. Did you forget about the dishes?
6. Do you think we have enough clean dishes for our dinner party tonight?
7. I'd like to use the sink to water my plants.
8. I hope the kitchen doesn't start to smell.

Notice that as we progress down the list, the speaker is less and less direct about what the spouse is actually supposed to do. In fact, the last two requests don't even mention dishes at all! Not only does it take more cognitive energy for the listener to discern what is being asked here, it is also more likely that the request will be misinterpreted, in one of two ways. First is a possible misunderstanding of content—perhaps the listener in example #6 above ("Do you think we have enough clean dishes for our dinner party tonight?") could think that the request is really for permission to buy more dishes, not to wash the existing dishes. Second is a possible misunderstanding of magnitude, or understanding how important the request is to the speaker. Let's take an example from a job negotiation. Due to our politeness reflex in making requests to a recruiter, instead of saying something definite along the lines of, "I need a schedule that starts at 9:00 a.m. daily," you might hedge your words a little bit to make the request seem more polite, and instead say something like, "If it's not too much trouble, starting closer to 9:00 a.m. would be better for me, if that's something that you can do."[10] Both requests in this example have clear content: the job candidate is requesting permission to start the workday at 9:00 a.m. But what differs is the intensity of the request. The second version makes it sound much less important to the job candidate than the first version does. By trying to be polite, the candidate may have inadvertently shot himself or herself in the foot by making it seem like a *want* and not a *need* to have that request accommodated. None of this is to say, of course, that politeness is something that you can set aside entirely. Even computers programmed to speak out loud with people need to have words such as "please" and "welcome" and "have a nice day" included because they are so important to human sensibilities.[11]

The most challenging problem associated with subordinate speech patterns is the fact that people typically do not know they are doing it. Not only do subordinates speak less clearly, they also use fewer words in total than do those with power. People tend to edit out what they feel won't be well received. Subordinates even use fewer gestures and express less emotion with their superiors than they do with their peers.[12] Even worse, the lower-power person is more likely to be experiencing negative emotions during the conversation. This reaction is logical, since it is a nerve-wracking experience to try and make requests in a job negotiation, remain polite and respectful, but still get your needs clearly on the table. Unfortunately, these negative emotions can also cloud both *what* is said and *how* it is said. Due to the fear of angering the higher-power person, people in the lower-power position often downplay their ideas and convictions.[13] Even the basic ways that people phrase questions or comments, along with their physical posture, can highlight deference to a more powerful other. Here are some examples of what's called "defensive communication" that might arise in a job negotiation:[14]

- Permission-asking: Using the construct "Is it OK with you if . . . ?" for too many ideas.
- Giving away power, decisions, ideas as theirs instead of yours: "Don't *you* think that . . . ?"
- Over-apologizing for ideas when it is not appropriate. Some people seem to use "I'm sorry" as a reflex or a filler.
- Coping humor, self-insults, and self-deprecation: "What do I know, I'm just . . . "

All of this adds up to the same basic problem. When we feel the other side has more power, we become overly cautious in our speech and thus run the risk of obscuring our true objectives. This makes the recruiter more likely to just fill in the content they misunderstood with their own ideas instead of truly understanding yours.[15] On top of that, it changes the way the recruiter judges you as a person. Job candidates using powerful language tend to be seen as more intelligent, attractive, competent and credible![16]

> **TIP**
>
> Make a conscious effort to make your requests in clear, unambiguous language. Otherwise, the unconscious tendency is to be indirect with those in power.

One explanation for why people use defensive communication so often is because lower-power people are more attentive to threats than to possible rewards. Thus, if a job candidate is more focused on the possibility of angering the hiring manager or even possibly having the job offer withdrawn, communication becomes much more fraught than if the candidate is focused on the possible rewards. In fact, facing a threat actually constrains our cognitive abilities (the "fight or flight" instinct in action). Thus, you would be well advised to frame the discussion as an opportunity for both sides to get something of value from each other, as opposed to a situation in which one must make requests from a higher authority.[17]

> **TIP**
>
> Think of the job negotiation as a balance between two sets of power: the recruiter's power to award the job, and your power to bring a solution to the recruiter's hiring needs.

LISTENING SKILLS

We started this chapter by noting that communicating well is hard work. In job negotiations, our natural communication tendencies tend to work against us. One of the reasons for this is that besides it being difficult to choose effective words to convey your messages, it's almost equally hard to listen effectively. Here's what happens in a typical challenging conversation, such as a job negotiation. You plan some ideas on what you're going to say. You get into the conversation, and the other person starts with a prologue whereby he or she starts by explaining what the options are going to be, what might be possible, etc. And what happens to you? You listen very closely to the first few things that are said, and then your mind tends to drift into thoughts of what it is that you wanted to remember to ask for, or how you wanted to phrase your request, or worse, you simply get distracted by noticing that the recruiter is wearing a blue shirt and it reminds you that you need to pick up your dry cleaning. Before you know it, you realize that the other person has been speaking for a while, *and you haven't been listening at all.* If you are like most people, this has happened to you, and probably not all that infrequently. It is like reading a book and realizing at the bottom of a page that you have not really absorbed anything that you just read. In that case, you can easily go back to the beginning and reread. In a real-time conversation, the moment—and the information that came with it—are both lost. What do you do? Most people try to cover for the lapse. They tune in again, focus strongly for a few seconds, and try to patch together what they missed.

This pattern also tends to emerge at another crucial point in the conversation, which is *right after you have asked an important question.* This seems even less likely—when you ask a question, you might be thinking, it is because you want to know the information and so of course you will listen to the answer! But sadly, all too often people do not listen well in this situation, either. You ask the question, and then your mind first *moves backward* to review how well you have asked this important question, and then *moves forward* to the next thing that you want to say, leaving out adequate focus on the present. It is not your fault. Our brains are just not wired all that well for listening. True active listening, where you are focused on nothing but absorbing the information being presented to you, is such hard work that our body temperature actually rises when we are engaged in it! This does not happen often in our daily lives. To address the difficulty of effective listening, psychologists in the field recommend a series of tools that together are called "reflective listening," where you recognize the other person's speech or directly repeat back key parts of information during the conversation to make sure that you are accurately absorbing what is being said. This is done by using one or more of the following six responses to the speaker:[18]

1. Affirming language (phrases such as "I see" and "Uh huh")
2. Paraphrasing ("What I understand your point to be is . . . ")
3. Clarifying the implicit ("It seems like you may also mean . . . ")
4. Reflecting core feelings ("It seems like this point is more important to you than the last?")

5. Silence (letting a few moments pass to internally reflect on what has been said)

6. Eye contact (too little and you lose the connection; too much and it makes the other person uncomfortable, but moderate direct eye contact is important).

TIP

Remember to listen. Motivate yourself by the realization that this is harder than it sounds: stop talking, stop thinking about other things or what you want to say next, and use reflective listening tools to focus yourself on the other person and only on what is being said right now.

SIDEBAR: DETECTING LIES

Part of effective listening is catching when the other person's statements might not be true. Unfortunately, it turns out that most of us are not very good lie detectors. Only those trained very carefully in reading minute changes to facial expressions tend to be better than random-chance guessers at figuring out who is lying. One of the reasons for this is that our expectations about how liars look when committing a falsehood are generally, well, false. But the belief that we can detect lies based on facial cues is so pervasive—even among those wishing to lie—that more people actually engage in lying on the telephone or in written text as opposed to face-to-face.[19] Also, not all lies are the same—complete falsehoods (such as a recruiter telling you that the company is actively interested in a second qualified candidate when no such person actually exists) are much more complicated and intimidating for people to use and pull off without giving away telltale signals that they are lying than are exaggerations (such as having the recruiter tell you that there is no possibility of getting the extra amount requested in salary when in fact there could be room to move). Here are some cues to detecting lies that have proven to be more reliable.

• Though we might expect liars to ramble as they tell a long and made-up story, in truth, liars tend to have *shorter* responses to questions.

- Liars tend to use higher pitch, more sentence corrections (such as "I mean . . ." or "that is . . ."), and they speak more slowly on average than do truth-tellers.[20]
- Liars use fewer personal pronouns (such as "I" or "we") and fewer complex sentences with connector words ("but" or "however"), and use more negative-emotion words.[21] These patterns are even easier to notice when communication is written as text as opposed to spoken out loud.
- Liars may tend to blink more and touch their faces more often (sometimes called the "Pinocchio Effect"; the theory is that the nose swells slightly when lying, causing one to need to touch or scratch it), though even knowing about these tendencies has not helped most people detect lies.[22]

The best tool in your toolbox for detecting lies, though, is asking questions. If you don't like, or trust, the answer you hear once, ask the question again in a different way. Bring up the same topic again but bundled differently and with different alternatives attached to it. Remember, your goal here is to get your needs met, not to uncover poor behavior from the other side. That being said, if you are sure that you are being lied to, that could offer you important information about the company and job you're considering!

To be effective speakers and listeners, we also need to understand the distinction between one-way and two-way communication. One-way communication is the type in which one person gives a lecture, for example, or sends a memo or letter, and the other side is supposed to receive the information. In truth, the speaker does not really know whether the listener has gotten the point or not. Two-way communication allows both parties to be speakers and listeners in turn, to ask clarifying questions, and to engage with each other's ideas—in other words, to have an actual conversation. Both styles have relative advantages and disadvantages, depending on the goals of the communication. For example, in the classroom, we sometimes do the following activity. A student volunteer (the speaker) is given a diagram of a complicated figure (a square resting on top of a diamond perched on top of a non-centered triangle, etc.) and is told to describe, using only words and not gestures or symbols, the figure such that the rest of the class (the listeners) can reproduce a drawing of the diagram on paper. This exercise is run twice in a row with two different geometric figures. One time, the audience of listeners is not allowed to speak or ask questions (they are told to imagine they are watching a lecture on TV), and the other time, the listeners are allowed to interact with the speaker, ask clarifying questions, and generally make the activity a conversation instead of a lecture. The first style represents one-way communication while the second represents two-way communication. Surprisingly, it does not matter if the one-way or the two-way style happens first. In the one-way version (the straight lecture), the speaker typically feels good about what he or she has presented, imagining the instructions to be crystal clear and straightforward by having delivered smooth and polished sentences. The audience, on the other hand, is usually frustrated by misunderstandings and confusion, and the resulting diagrams are almost always wrong, much to the surprise of the speaker. In the two-way version (the conversation), the speaker typically becomes increasingly flummoxed by the questions, surprised that things did not make sense the first time, and tries reframing the instructions in new ways, often delivering a choppy, complicated series of answers. Yet over a longer time frame (it often takes more than twice as long to complete the two-way version), consensus is reached, and in the end, a much larger percentage of the listeners have actually managed to draw the correct figure. What is learned in this exercise? One-way communication (the straight lecture) is better at two things: it is more efficient, and it allows the speaker to maintain control and thus deliver a more eloquent and satisfying set of ideas. However, it is less effective at actually conveying information than is the two-way conversational process. People learn better when they are part of the conversation, especially when they can explain key points in their own words.

TIP

Engage in the conversation with the recruiter. Make sure you restate the key points and ideas presented by the other side.

THREE ADDITIONAL TIPS FOR EFFECTIVE COMMUNICATION IN JOB NEGOTIATIONS

First, do not forget to take a break from the conversation (if necessary, by leaving the room) and check whether you are covering what you need to cover by asking your questions and truly understanding the answers that are given. It is always reasonable to ask for a moment to review what has been covered thus far. Along these lines, make sure you feel that the other side not only heard what it is that you wanted to say, but understood which things were the more important elements to you.

TIP

Take a break to regroup your thoughts and review whether the communication has been effective.

Second, as a corollary to our discussion of how hard it is to listen, don't forget that the other side is having just as hard a time listening to you. Think about it this way—if you had to hand off a critical task at work to a peer, how would you make sure that he or she truly understood what had to be done? How many times would you want to walk through the instructions? Would you rely on doing so once, or would you want to follow up the conversation with a written memo detailing the highlights? And/or, would you respectfully ask the person to explain it back to you to make sure the message was received? The rule of thumb is that to ensure that you have gotten a message across to anybody under any circumstances, you want to send the same information multiple times and in multiple ways. Your chances of common understanding increase substantially with this process.

TIP

If it's important, say it twice! For example, follow up phone calls with an e-mail highlighting key points.

Third, remember to stay calm and confident. Another unconscious rule of thumb we tend to use without thinking about it is that "confident speakers probably do know what they are talking about."[23] Anxiety causes people to stutter, pause, repeat themselves, lose track of the conversation, and engage in less eye contact. Also know that people in a good mood are more persuasive than others, so keep yourself in a good frame of mind, and take a break when you find that you are losing your good mood.[24]

TIP

Confidence sells. Practice elements of your conversation ahead of time to be more confident in what you are trying to say.

SUMMARY

Communicating well with your recruiter is one of the most powerful tools you have for job negotiation success. Here are some of the key concepts we discussed that can make you more effective in your communication:

- Explain things clearly—don't assume that the person you are talking with has the same knowledge that you do. Don't be afraid to ask for clarification when you don't understand something.
- You can be more persuasive by understanding some basic principles and putting them to work for you in practical ways:
  - Scarcity—highlight your uniqueness.
  - Authority—list your degrees and expertise.
  - Liking—be positive and associate yourself with positive outcomes.
  - Social proof—let them know that others are interested in you as well.
  - Commitment and consistency—have the recruiter acknowledge interest in you and that you would be a good match for the position.
  - Reciprocity—Make concessions in order to gain on other, more important points.
- Be polite, but clear and unambiguous. Avoid defensive communication. Remember that you have the power to bring a solution to the recruiter by offering your unique and qualified services.
- Listen carefully! Practice reflective listening to ensure that all information is being communicated effectively. Restate things until all parties understand them.

NOTES

1. Friestadand, M., and P. Wright, The persuasion knowledge model: How people cope with persuasion attempts. *Journal of Consumer Research*, 21, 1994: 1–31.

2. Thompson, L., *Organizational behavior today*. Upper Saddle River, NJ: Pearson Prentice Hall, 2008.

3. Cialdini, R. B., *Influence: Science and practice*. Boston: Allyn and Bacon, 2001.

4. Brehm, J. W., *A theory of psychological reactance*. Academic Press, 1966.

5. Cialdini, *Influence*.

6. Razran, G. H. S., Conditioning away social bias by the luncheon technique. *Psychological Bulletin*, 37, 1938: 481.

7. Cialdini, *Influence*.

8. Brown, P., and S. C. Levinson, *Politeness: Some universals in language use*. Cambridge, England: Cambridge University Press, 1987.

9. Adapted from Krauss, R. M., and S. R. Fussell, Social psychological models of interpersonal communication. In *Social Psychology: Handbook of basic principles*, E. T. Higgins and A. W. Kruglanski, Editors, 655–701. New York: Guilford, 1996.

10. Moreland, D. A., Language and power: An empirical analysis of linguistic strategies used in superior-subordinate communication. *Journal of Organizational Behavior*, 21, 2000: 235–248.

11. Ibid.

12. Hall, J. A., et al., Attributing the sources of accuracy in unequal-power dyadic communication: Who is better and why? *Journal of Experimental Social Psychology*, 42, 2006: 18–27.

13. Anderson, C., and J. L. Berdahl, The experience of power: Examining the effects of power on approach and inhibition tendencies. *Journal of Personality and Social Psychology*, 83, 2002: 1362–1377.

14. Nelson, D. L., and J. C. Quick, *Organizational behavior: Foundations, realities, and challenges*. 4th ed. Australia: Thomson-Southwestern, 2003.

15. Sparks, J. R., and C. S. Areni, Style versus substance: Multiple roles of language power in persuasion. *Journal of Applied Social Psychology*, 38, 2008: 37–60.

16. Bradac, J. J., and A. Mulac, Attributional consequences of powerful and powerless speech styles in a crisis-intervention context. *Journal of Language and Social Psychology*, 3, 1984: 1–19.

17. Anderson and Berdahl, The experience of power.

18. Nelson and Quick, *Organizational behavior*.

19. DePaulo, B. M., et al., Lying in everyday life. *Journal of Personality and Social Psychology*, 70, 1996: 979–995.

20. Ekman, P., *Telling lies: Clues to deceit in the marketplace, politics, and marriage*. 3rd ed. New York: Norton, 2001.

21. Newman, M. L., et al., Lying words: Predicting deception from linguistic styles. *Personality and Social Psychology Bulletin*, 29, 2003: 665–675.

22. Navarro, J., *What every BODY is saying*. New York: Harper Collins, 2008.

23. Dillard, J. P., and L. J. Marshall, Persuasion as a social skill. In *Handbook of Communication and Social Interaction Skills*, J. O. Green and B. R. Burleson, Editors, 479–513 (see particularly page 495). Mahwah, NJ: Lawrence Erlbaum, 2003.

24. Ibid.

SIX

Negotiating via E-mail: You May Need to Do This, So Do It Right

Few would disagree that face-to-face communication is very effective relative to other forms, including telephone calls, e-mails, and text messages. Unfortunately, it is not always practical in today's fast-paced and geographically dispersed world to count on face-to-face interaction for an entire job negotiation. Instead, a considerable amount of communication in a job negotiation may now occur electronically, such as via e-mail. While face-to-face and phone communication have long formed the backbone of job negotiations, over the past decade, an increasing number of people now combine these traditional modes of communication with e-mail. Not surprisingly, each mode of communication has advantages and disadvantages. While you may not be able to choose how you communicate with your potential employer, it will benefit you to understand how e-mail communication can (often unknowingly) change a person's behavior and how to safeguard yourself against typical mistakes. Likewise, knowing the advantages of e-mail communication will allow you to make the most of this opportunity. Hence, in this chapter, we review both the potential advantages and disadvantages of negotiating via e-mail and offer strategies to help you navigate this process.

COMMUNICATION BANDWIDTH

Before we review the pros and cons of job negotiations via e-mail, it is important to understand the critical role that nonverbal communication plays in getting your message across to another party. Nonverbal communication is part of the communication bandwidth for a particular medium, and describes the types of cues available (gestures, tone of voice, etc.) to the sender and receiver of a message. Verbal communication entails the explicit words that transpire, while nonverbal communication is anything that is not an *explicit* word. You may ask whether such cues are actually important for understanding one another; the answer is yes, and overwhelmingly so. Some experts have estimated that as much as 90 percent of the meaning in one's message can be understood without actually hearing any of the words spoken, just by looking at the person's gestures, hearing the tone of voice, and looking at facial expressions.[1] Loud, fast speech, for instance, may lead you to assume that the speaker is nervous or agitated. In other words, a considerable amount of the message is conveyed through the nonverbal element.

Imagine that you are negotiating a potential job offer after you had already committed to future vacation plans. Not wanting to call and bother the hiring manager, you send a request via e-mail to take those dates off for your personal vacation time. The e-mail reply you get back is a simple line of text saying merely "That's just great." Was this an acceptance of your request, or was it a signal of frustration regarding the request? It is difficult to tell because you lack the nonverbal contextual cues such as tone of voice and facial expressions that would accompany the response if you were face-to-face.

One of the most important types of nonverbal cues that people use in spoken conversation with others is called paralanguage, which describes vocalized sounds that are not real words, such as "uh huh" and "mm-hmmm," to convey understanding. These are so critical in spoken conversation that when we do an exercise in class in which students have to listen to a peer speak in a small group *without* being able to utter any sounds such as "uh huh" in response, not only do both speakers and listeners find the experience frustrating, but listeners even have a harder time understanding the basic concepts of what the speaker is trying to convey.

One of the ways to describe what is lost when progressing from (1) face-to-face interaction, to (2) phone conversations, to (3) text-only e-mail is nuance. It becomes harder to "read" the other person as you proceed from (1) to (3). People even tend to unintentionally mirror the way the other person acts in spoken conversations,[2] helping to explain why people feel most comfortable interacting with someone whom they can see and speak to out loud, and why people tend to cooperate more in that context. In fact, an entire catalog of symbols has evolved in an effort to address this shortcoming in text-only communication: emoticons.

Emoticons are symbols such as those smiley-face punctuation marks, :-), that are supposed to indicate tone of voice—to show that one is joking, for example, or sympathetic, or teasing. While emoticons can be very effective, most professionals agree that the place for those types of symbols remains in personal exchanges rather than in professional ones. As the current generation of young adults, raised on texting as a standard means of communication, becomes dominant in the workplace, this may change. Will the next generation adapt to the current standards of professional communication, or will it someday become acceptable to "text-wink" at your boss? Time will tell, but for now, it is unlikely that you will be able to rely on emoticons to get your point across.

As you will see from our discussion below, we recommend that job negotiations be done face-to-face whenever possible. Face-to-face communication, with the widest bandwidth for cues, gives you the best chance at sending and receiving messages accurately, with phone calls in second place. But realizing that face-to-face job negotiations are not always an option, for the remainder of this chapter, we will explore how negotiating via e-mail, *with its inherent lack of nonverbal cues*, can help or hinder your job negotiations, and present tips for how to put your best foot forward when using e-mail in a job negotiation.

A TRUE STORY

Don was a personable guy, and a very animated speaker who thrived on engaging other people in conversation. But when he was on the market, one company was doing first-round interviews over e-mail to save money. Don says of the experience, "First, I felt like I was signing up for an online dating service, and had a hard time describing myself in writing. Second, I felt like everything I said was so flat and boring and I couldn't express my personal side, and it must have come across that way to the company too, since I wasn't called in for the next round."

ADVANTAGES OF E-MAIL

Typically, e-mail use in job negotiations is reserved for the counteroffer phase. There are three main advantages to having some part of your negotiation happen over e-mail. The first and most obvious is the convenience aspect, whether you are across the street or in a different time zone. There is currently no better option for busy people. Being able to think, write, and respond in your own time instead of having to coordinate with another person is so valuable that online text-based communication seems to be here to stay.

You yourself have probably had the experience of seeing an important e-mail and then deciding to wait until you can give it your full attention before you read it, or read it well. Once you decide to devote your time and attention to it, you are also able to read and reread it, think about it, process your initial reaction before you need to respond, consult with others on how to respond if desired, think through and draft responses to review again later with fresh eyes, and generally be much more careful than you ever get to be in a simultaneous real-time conversation. Since this flexibility allows for more focus on what is being said and also on how to respond, there is even a school of thought that says that professional feedback should all be given via e-mail. This would allow the recipient the chance to react first emotionally and then cognitively without the need for regulating that process or defending oneself to the speaker in real time,[3] though people may also feel slighted if the boss decides to e-mail feedback to employees instead of speaking to them face-to-face.[4] In all, the convenience factor allows you to attend to and deliver messages in your own time.

Another advantage is the built-in "paper" trail. E-mail automatically keeps a record of every detail in the conversation for either side to refer back to as needed. This is especially handy if the negotiations are complex, or are spread out over a significant period of time. The written format may also allow for the presentation of more ideas, and more complex ideas, in an organized fashion than an unstructured spoken conversation would. E-mail is an excellent medium for presenting detailed information since it can be a lot to absorb if presented out loud.

A TRUE STORY

Aileen was negotiating for her employment package over e-mail with the hiring manager. When the written contract came from HR, it had a lower salary number than had been promised. Since she had saved the e-mail exchange, she was able to correct this mistake with HR herself without having to interrupt the hiring manager for clarification.

The third advantage is something that is not always obvious. It turns out that people notice status and power differences *less* in an online context than when facing each other. For example, someone who might be incredibly hesitant to speak up in front of the boss is much more likely to share

Table 6.1. Summary of Advantages of E-mail in Job Negotiations

1. Convenience	You communicate on your schedule.
2. Time to craft responses	You can edit the message until you get it just right.
3. Record keeping	You can go back and retrieve details of the discussion.
4. Power differences reduced	Intimidation is reduced online versus face-to-face.

ideas when the discussion circulates virtually.[5] This is potentially advantageous in job negotiations in which people are at least a little intimidated by the recruiter. E-mailing may allow you to freely share your ideas more thoroughly than you might have if you were only having spoken conversations. A related advantage of e-mail communication is that it allows you to level the playing field if you feel that the other side is presenting information that you are not familiar with, because you get a chance to do your homework on these new features of an offer before responding. Table 6.1 summarizes the advantages of using e-mail for communicating.

DISADVANTAGES OF E-MAIL

The potential disadvantage list for e-mail, unfortunately, is longer and more complicated. The most glaring limitation is the potential for misunderstanding. Absent nonverbal cues and the chance to ask clarifying questions in real time, e-mail negotiations can sometimes get misinterpreted and lead to faulty assumptions about the issues being discussed. In fact, though e-mail messages often feel long and difficult to follow, the average interaction contains less actual dialogue than the average face-to-face conversation on the same task.[6] The text words are harder to choose and take more time to spell out than to speak aloud, and so people end up saying less and getting less ground covered in terms of the details. The burden is on you to follow up with clarifying questions, either in writing or out loud—this is especially important since people are generally *less* likely to ask good diagnostic questions when they communicate via e-mail, as well as are less likely to do an adequate job sharing good information about their own true interests.[7]

A TRUE STORY

Due to a typo in an e-mail from the HR representative, Marty was accidentally sent to the wrong place for his interview. By the time the mistake was realized and he ran across town to make it for the last 30 minutes of the hour-long interview, he felt out of sorts and rushed, and did not put his best foot forward. Even though the mistake was theirs, it made him look bad. He was sure that had the arrangements been made verbally out loud, he would have double-checked the location instead of assuming that the e-mail message was correct.

Next, in addition to misunderstanding the content itself in e-mail, people often misunderstand the intentions of the other side, especially when it comes to delays. This is in part because our society seems to have developed an "it can wait" attitude about information and questions presented in e-mails that does not apply equally to verbal conversations. For example, what do you consider to be an acceptable delay in responding to an e-mail? By the end of the day? Within 24 hours, or 48 hours? Imagine that you send your recruiter a message with questions about the offer that you received. A day goes by and you do not hear back. Was your message even received, let alone read? Is it being looked into, which might require some behind-the-scenes checking on the part of the other side? Were any of your requests unreasonable such that the recruiter now simply does not feel like answering you? In online interactions, one is frequently left in the dark with silence or delayed responses, and people often tend to assume the worst about the cause for the silence. In a verbal phone conversation, you would likely be able to get some information back regarding the next steps and probably the timeline as well. You might even sense some push-back if your questions did not please the other side. Any of these responses give you some additional information, whereas complete silence on e-mail provides you with none.

You may also face the issue of incomplete responses. If you have asked a number of questions in an e-mail, you may find yourself in a position where you received responses to a few of the issues you raised, but not to all of them. This is common in e-mail, where the responder is able to pick and choose the questions they wish to address and ignore the rest in their reply. But you are left in an uncomfortable position. Do you assume that the other answers are still to come? Or that they were overlooked, and perhaps you should gently remind the recruiter of these issues? Or should you assume that the omission is a signal that the requests were denied?

Misunderstandings can also spring from a misreading of your intended tone. More specifically, your requests via e-mail may come across as being more definite and inflexible than you intended them to be. Without the chance to add tone and watch the reaction of the other side, these kinds of misunderstandings abound in e-mail job negotiations. Or worse, your e-mail gets forwarded to someone whom you have never met and has even less chance of understanding the tone with which you have asked your questions or made your requests.

A TRUE STORY

Suzanne sent an e-mail to her hiring manager asking about the possibility of working internationally at some point. She was trying to feel out the potential for international opportunities for someone in her position. But the recruiter misunderstood her tone and lost the nuance of her "just feeling this out" request. Instead, he jumped to the incorrect conclusion that Suzanne was trying to get an overseas assignment instead of the local job she was originally hired to fill, and set about making the request for her internally. Though they were able to clear up the misunderstanding before she found herself either out of the job or packing for foreign lands, she felt it hurt her credibility to have to backpedal and remove her "request" once it had been passed around inside the company. In her words, "it made me feel like a flake!"

E-mails also don't always get the same degree of attention as similar information would if presented face-to-face. We live in an age in which there are many competing demands for your attention at every moment, and it is common for people to try to do and think about multiple things for much of the day. Despite assurances from people who constantly multitask that they can handle the information overload, it is a fact that people absorb significantly less information when they are trying to attend to more than one thing simultaneously. In fact, chronic multitaskers are actually *worse* at absorbing information from any one source than are people who multitask less frequently.[8] For this reason, and given that many people review multiple e-mails in rapid succession, or read e-mails while working on another task (even while engaging in a meeting or other conversation), your message runs the risk of not getting across very effectively. (This holds true for any stage of acquiring a new job, from trying to get your foot in the door to fine-tuning the offer at the end stage).

A TRUE STORY

Steve really wanted a position posted within his company, but in a different city from his current job. He reached out to the hiring manager numerous times via e-mail. Finally, fed up with the lack of response, and at our advice, he flew at his own expense to the city and invited the hiring manager to meet over a cup of coffee at her convenience. The hiring manager was impressed with Steve's initiative and agreed to meet with him. After the face-to-face introduction, his resume was given the attention it deserved and he ended up being offered a desirable position in the city he wanted. In the end, his investment in airfare to overcome the hurdles of e-mail communication paid off many times over.

Yet another distinct disadvantage to take into account with e-mail is that people sometimes act more negatively online than they do when communicating through other channels. For one, people tend to lie more online—especially when they have something direct to gain from the lie. In a classroom exercise, for example, MBA students were told that they were allotted a particular sum of money and that they had a partner with whom they needed to share the money. They were also told that the partner would *never know* the actual size of the pot to be divided, nor would they *ever know* who their partner was (that is, the exercise was anonymous). They then were asked to fill out a form to send to their anonymous partner, indicating the total amount of money in the pot to be divided as well as how much they were allocating to them (the other party). The catch was that half of the people filled out their form on a piece of paper, while the other half filled out their form as an online attachment. Interestingly, most of the participants (more than half) in this exercise lied regardless of how they communicated the information. When asked to fill out an actual pen-and-paper form, approximately 60 percent of people told the other side a false figure for the pot size. For example, instead of telling the partner that there was $89 total available, one might report that there was only $60 available and allocate $30 to the other side—to make it seem nice and fair while pocketing $59 ($89–$30). But the biggest surprise was that when people filled out the identical form online (versus pen-and-paper), the number of people who lied jumped to 92 percent. That is to say, *nearly everybody* lied in the online condition. Shocking! In another version of this exercise, participants were told that both their identities and any false information they provided *would* be revealed in the very next class. It did not change a thing. People lied just as often, and still lied more often online.[9]

Why do people tend to lie more online? To begin to formulate an answer, we need to review a few other interesting behaviors that occur when communication moves online. For one, when people do a peer-evaluation task online versus doing it on paper, those online give systematically *lower* ratings on average, even when evaluating the exact same person.[10] In addition, people are more likely to use negative language with each other online (an effect called "flaming"),[11] are less likely to cooperate with their group-members,[12] and feel more justified acting in a more self-serving manner when interacting online.[13] Taken together, we start to see a consistent pattern in which people seem to give themselves more license to act negatively toward others when communicating online as opposed to communicating in other ways. Most agree that physical distance and the inability to directly see how our behaviors are affecting others contribute to this trend.[14] Regardless of the causal mechanisms, it is important to realize that these negative behaviors exist in order to more effectively avoid this potentially dangerous situation. The clear message for you in the midst of a job negotiation is to not make requests via e-mail, since your message may not be given the attention it deserves and may get a more negative response.

TIP

Don't use e-mail in a job negotiation if you have a choice. Take the initiative and make the effort to meet in person, or at least pick up the phone.

Yet another problematic area in e-mail job negotiations is that researchers have found that online negotiators have a more difficult time reaching an agreement than they would with a face-to-face conversation.[15] This is likely because in addition to the more negative tone and more negative (and self-serving) behavior that we have discussed already, e-mail communication can also inspire impatience with the process. You have probably recognized this common situation yourself, when after a few back-and-forths over e-mail, the process feels tedious and both sides just want it to be over.

In the face of all the convenience that e-mail affords, it actually tends to take *longer* to negotiate via e-mail. Each time you send a message, you are ready to think about the issue. But then you need to set it aside until you get a response, by which point you need to find the time once again to devote your full attention to the matter, and remind yourself of the details covered thus far. There also tends to be a sense of reciprocity about the timing of e-mail exchanges—if the other side took a full 24 hours to get back to you, you are going to feel comfortable taking 24 hours as well. All this adds up to a disconnected process that takes more time than it should online versus face-to-face. People also consistently report feeling decreased levels of trust and decreased feelings of fairness with the process when interacting online. They cooperate with each other less, and are more likely to throw out risky options (and even make riskier final decisions) than they would be face-to-face.[16]

A TRUE STORY

Kevin lived on the East Coast and was approached by a small business owner in California about taking a job for which he would not relocate but would work remotely. Their entire negotiation was conducted over e-mail (the owner preferred e-mail to phone calls so he could consider his words carefully). After several back-and-forths, Kevin was prepared to take the job; but then the owner threw him a curveball and told him that since the position was new, he wanted to hire Kevin for only a 90-day trial period. Kevin argued that the new position was an investment, and the owner could not expect to see the kind of results he hoped for in less than a year. Although the owner did agree with this point and told Kevin he was prepared to accept the terms, he continued to refer to the job as "an experiment." The job negotiation was dropped for some time as both parties were frustrated with the language being used by the other. Finally Kevin picked up the phone and was able explain to the business owner that he objected to the use of the word "experiment," only to find out that the business owner had originally considered his own marriage an "experiment" and thus used that word for any new venture! They were able to settle on mutually acceptable terms with a review after three months and a more realistic set of goals for the time period. In retrospect, Kevin was frustrated with the misunderstanding that e-mail had caused, almost costing him the job, but was grateful for the fact that all of his employment terms were in writing so that his review could, and did, go smoothly at the three-month mark.

TIP

When in doubt about the content of an e-mail, pick up the phone to clarify areas of confusion.

Table 6.2 summarizes the disadvantages associated with e-mail use.

Table 6.2.   Summary of Disadvantages of E-mail in Job Negotiations

1. Misunderstandings	Lack of body language and tonal inflections makes misunderstandings more likely.
2. Less dialogue	Often leaves important elements or explanations unsaid, or gives incomplete responses.
3. Takes more time	Frustrating to keep reimmersing yourself in topic.
4. Less importance	People put messages off for later or dash off responses.
5. Responses are more negative	Less inhibition, harsher words and opinions.

STRATEGIES FOR SUCCESS WITH E-MAIL

With the convenience of e-mail being a strong advantage, how does one navigate around the various drawbacks? This section covers tips and strategies to help you maintain clarity and effective communication when negotiating via e-mail. Though it should go without saying, the first and most important point is to make sure you use appropriate language and grammar so that your e-mail reflects your most professional self. Next and perhaps less obvious is to make sure you have reached out to connect face-to-face with the person you are dealing with before you start negotiating electronically. Most often, by the time you get to the e-mail exchange of details in a job contract, you will have already met in person. If you have not, then you should try to have had some sort of conversation with the other person before leaping into the "all business" part, to break the ice. Research has shown that this can tremendously increase the likelihood of successful agreements.

In one study, participants were told to exchange one e-mail with just pleasantries before starting a negotiation with a stranger. Though the pair only told each other superficial things about themselves in this exchange (where they were each from, what their areas of expertise were, and sometimes something about one hobby or interest outside of work), it was amazing to see how often both sides used these bits of information throughout the exchanges. For example, one person mentioned that he was an avid golfer. Throughout the rest of the e-mail exchange, the other side made comments referring to this, such as, "We're having fine weather out here, I bet you'd be hitting the links today if you were here!" and the like. And, those pairs that did engage in this type of pre-negotiation exchange were more likely to build rapport and, most importantly, reached agreement more often than those who skipped this step.[17] An initial phone call between negotiators before negotiating online also serves to break the ice in this way.[18]

Yet another tool (albeit a potentially risky tool) that can work as an effective icebreaker in e-mail negotiations is humor. Those who sent a cartoon to the other side at the beginning of an e-mail negotiation in our classes were more likely to reach agreement than were those who did not.[19] But, humor can be slippery, and it is sometimes difficult to predict what other people will find funny, particularly if you do not know them and cannot even see them. In fact, when we did that exercise, we had to search long and hard for a cartoon that was relevant to negotiations, not offensive in any way, and still humorous to at least most of the people we checked with! So even though this strategy might have a time and place, the job negotiation is probably not it.

Another, more subtle tactic is to attempt to humanize the interaction. Most people like to interact with other people, and one of the dangers of the e-mailing process is the dehumanization of the other party. You want to try to reintroduce human elements into the conversation as much as possible without being too awkward about it. For example, you do not want to say: "I'm hoping we can talk about the starting salary figure, and by the way, have I told you that I like to swim on the weekends?" That will probably not flow naturally for you or the other side. Nor would a sentence such as "So, Bob, tell me a little bit about yourself before we get to the hard details" be a big success here. Instead, the more subtle but successful approach is to work in some questions that allow you to introduce yourself. What if you said, "I do have a few follow-up questions on the package details you sent me previously. In addition, I was wondering if you know anything about where there are pools or swim clubs nearby— I used to swim in college and still try to make that a part of my routine. Does the company have contacts at a local gym?" Even if the area of discussion does not make it into the final negotiation, in the text-only context, it is that much more important to make sure people still feel like people, and furnishing the other side with some details about your life in an appropriate way can help serve this purpose.

TIP

When negotiating via text, try to reach out to the other side with small details that make the conversation more human to help facilitate reaching agreement.

TOP 10 RULES FOR E-MAIL SUCCESS

In terms of the mechanics of using e-mail text to present yourself and your ideas, we have compiled a top 10 list of rules for e-mail success to provide additional help in managing this part of the job negotiation most effectively.

- *Rule 1: Be complete but not overwhelming in content.* Make sure you provide enough detail to avoid misunderstandings of any kind, but not so much text that what you are saying gets lost in large paragraphs. Text is hard to skim on a screen, especially now that people often read their messages on tiny handheld devices. Too much text can work against you. Admit it—you also don't like it when someone sends you long and rambling e-mails. Be concise.

- *Rule 2: Organize text accessibly.* Part of the too-much-text problem described above is poorly organized text. Don't forget that text is a visual medium, and you need to make sure what you are saying can jump out at the reader. Avoid long paragraphs, fancy fonts, or complicated formatting that is likely to get lost in the e-translation.

- *Rule 3: Use numbered lists.* There is nothing worse than writing a long e-mail with four main questions in it, and getting a response to only two of them, as we described earlier. If you start the e-mail with a very clear statement that includes the scope of your inquiries, you are much more likely to keep the other person's attention on each of your issues. For example: "I'm writing today because I have four areas I would like to ask about," and then proceed with your numbered list of four things. This at least increases the odds that all four items will hit the radar screen of the reader, who hopefully will then address them all in response. Needless to say, there is a limit to the effectiveness of this process: "I have questions on 14 different issues" is not likely to win you any friends! Five or six items (at most) per e-mail are a reasonable limit on what's appropriate to ask for from the reader.

- *Rule 4: Present options*. Within your numbered lists, you can help the reader respond by proving options embedded within the requests. Especially if you are asking for terms to be negotiable, this is a great time to preemptively offer various options for trading some things off for other things, as we discussed in Chapter 4.

- *Rule 5: Invite suggestions and build in opportunities for feedback*. You will not have the advantage of reading the other person's face or body cues when you ask to negotiate items, so you may need to go out of your way to ask whether you are on solid ground or not. Even general comments such as "Your thoughts on this idea would be greatly appreciated" may draw the other person out to give you some of the feedback you will need to proceed effectively.

- *Rule 6: Be clear about what you want in return*. Are you hoping for just some sense, or are you looking for a concrete counteroffer? Either way, it is best to try to be clear with the other side about whether you are just checking on information, or establishing an actual request that you would like them to respond to with a yes-no or a counteroffer.

- *Rule 7: Pay attention to the process*. If you know that there will be a delay or a time when you are not able to check your messages or respond, be sure to let the other side know ahead of time. On the other hand, be patient with reasonable delays from the other side.

- *Rule 8: Pay attention to the details*. Don't ever hit "send" without rereading your message at least once and making sure the details are all as they should be. You will also want to watch all the cues that you are sending, not just the words themselves. For instance, what does it mean if you type in all capital letters? Some people say that this just indicates emphasis; others think it means you are shouting. Make sure your messages are free of ambiguities like that. And *of course* grammar, spelling, and correct punctuation are important. You are representing your professional image here.

- *Rule 9: Paraphrase*. For many reasons, people are likely to miss what you are trying to say. Make sure you say things in clear and simple ways, and then reiterate them again where appropriate. Also, paraphrase what you believe the other side to have said to make sure you have understood the incoming messages and offers as well.

- *Rule 10: Pick up the phone if you feel you need to*. Messages have a better chance of getting through if the same message is sent multiple times and in multiple ways. If you get the feeling that e-mail communication is potentially causing problems, schedule a phone call to talk out loud about the points in question.

SUMMARY

While face-to-face communication generally allows people to communicate more effectively than with words alone, the extra time you have to consider offers and responses when negotiations happen over e-mail offers some advantages as well. While we recommend doing job negotiations face-to-face whenever possible, chances are that you may have to conduct at least part of your job negotiation through e-mail. When relying on e-mail, remember the impediments to this form of communication—people tend to use fewer words, to lie more, to pay less attention to what they read, to misinterpret tone, and to be more negative. You can be much more successful and effective communicating with e-mail if you remember to:

- Maintain a human connection with the other party.
- Be complete, concise, and clear.
- Format your text for readability and ease of response.
- Don't hesitate to take the initiative and pick up the phone or ask for a meeting when necessary.

NOTES

1. Mehrabian, A., *Silent messages*. Belmont, CA: Wadsworth, 1971.
2. Drolet, A. L., and M. W. Morris, Rapport in conflict resolution: Accounting for how face-to-face contact fosters mutual cooperation in mixed-motive conflicts. *Journal of Experimental Social Psychology*, 36, 2000: 26–50.
3. Kluger, A. N., and A. DeNisi, The effects of feedback intervention on performance: A historical review, a meta-analysis, and a preliminary feedback theory. *Psychological Bulletin*, 119, 1996: 254–284.

4. Kurtzberg, T. R., L. Y. Belkin, and C. E. Naquin, The effect of e-mail on attitude towards performance feedback. *International Journal of Organizational Analysis*, 14(1), 2006: 4–21.

5. Sproull, L., and S. Kiesler, *Connections: New ways of working in the networked organization*. Cambridge, MA: MIT Press, 1991.

6. Thompson, L., and J. Nadler, Negotiating via information technology: Theory and application. *Journal of Social Issues*, 58, 2002: 109–124.

7. Nadler, J., and D. Shestowsky, Negotiation, information technology, and the problem of the faceless other. In *Negotiation Theory and Research*, edited by L. Thompson, 146–172. 2006.

8. Ophir, E., C. Nass, and A. Wagner, Cognitive control in media multitaskers. *Proceedings of the National Academy of Sciences*, 106, 2009: 15521–15522.

9. Naquin, C. E., T. R. Kurtzberg, and L. Y. Belkin, The finer points of lying online: E-mail versus paper-and-pen. *Journal of Applied Psychology*, 95(2), 2010: 387–394.

10. Kurtzberg, T. R., C. E. Naquin, and L. Belkin, Electronic performance appraisals: The effects of e-mail communication on peer ratings in actual and simulated environments. *Organizational Behavior and Human Decision Processes*, 98, 2005: 216–226.

11. Kiesler, S., and L. Sproull, Response effects in the electronic survey. *Public Opinion Quarterly*, 50, 1986: 402–413.

12. Naquin, C. E., T. R. Kurtzberg, and L. Y. Belkin, E-mail communication and group cooperation in mixed motive contexts. *Social Justice Research*, 21, 2008: 470–489.

13. Naquin, Kurtzberg, and Belkin, The finer points of lying online.

14. Sproull, L., and S. Kiesler, Reducing social context cues: Electronic mail in organizational communication. *Management Science*, 32, 1986: 1492–1512.

15. Moore, D. A., et al., Long and short routes to success in electronically mediated negotiation: Group affiliations and good vibrations. *Organizational Behavior and Human Decision Processes*, 77(1), 1999: 22–43.

16. McGuire, T. W., S. Kiesler, and J. Siegel, Group and computer mediated discussion effects in risk decision making. *Journal of Personality and Social Psychology*, 52(5), 1987: 917–930.

17. Moore, et al., Long and short routes to success in electronically mediated negotiation.

18. Morris, M. W., et al., Schmooze or lose: Social friction and lubrication in e-mail negotiations. *Group Dynamics: Theory, Research, and Practice*, 6(1), 2002: 89–100.

19. Kurtzberg, T. R., C. E. Naquin, and L. Y. Belkin, Humor as a relationship-building tool in online deal making. *International Journal of Conflict Management*, 20(4), 2009: 377–397.

SEVEN

Headhunters

HOW HEADHUNTERS WORK

The majority of professionals represent themselves in a job negotiation, but in some instances, you may have a headhunter from an executive search firm, or another kind of intermediary, bargain on your behalf in the job negotiation. In this chapter, we talk about the pros and cons of working with such intermediaries, their motivations, and the best strategies for you to use in these circumstances. Let's start with a quick look at what a headhunter actually does.

Often working under the name of executive search firms, headhunting is sometimes described as "matchmaking," because a headhunter's job is to work on behalf of a particular hiring firm to find suitable candidates to fill specific openings. Executive search firms keep a large database of resumes in order to identify candidates who would likely complement their client's corporate culture and strategic plan. Information on these candidates is then submitted to their clients for selection. Executive search firms also might do prescreening interviews along with reference and background checks. Most headhunters specialize in a particular industry, and some are even more specialized into a certain type of skill set or expertise. Part of the headhunter's job is to tell the candidate about the firm, but their primary objective is to find suitable candidates for the firm. The more specialized the job, the more likely a firm is to use a headhunter to do the work of creating a list of qualified applicants.

Headhunters get paid in one of three ways. In "full-retainer" searches, the headhunter (or firm) is paid for the job whether or not they actually find someone to fill the spot. "Partial retainer" payment means that the headhunter receives an up-front fee of perhaps $5–10K, and then the rest is paid when a candidate is hired. The third and most common mechanism for payment is called "contingency," whereby the headhunter does not get paid until the position is filled, and then is paid a percentage of the annual salary (and sometimes benefits) of the signed contract. The percentage paid out can typically range anywhere from 20 to 33 percent, but generally hovers around 25 percent.

Why would executives at a company decide to spend many thousands of dollars on a headhunter when they can just promote internally or find someone themselves? This is a good question, and one that every single hiring manager also tends to ask. In fact, headhunters report that they are usually brought in as a last resort. An open position is typically considered first as an in-house opportunity to promote or shift someone who already works in the company either by selection or internal posting. That is the most painless route to filling the position for the company. If that fails, the second approach is usually to see who knows someone personally on the outside who might be a good fit and potentially interested. If that also does not result in a match, the company next may post an ad on its own website and solicit resumes from the open market. If no suitable candidates are forthcoming or several interviews have not resulted in a good match, the hiring manager typically begins to realize that the open spot is costing the company money directly in terms of lost productivity, sales, etc., and is perhaps even starting to snowball into backing up the work of several other individuals. Even if the consequences are not directly financial, somebody may be doing two people's work, and this is unsustainable over extended periods of time. At some point, the hiring manager crosses a threshold of pain (financially based, stress-based, or both) whereby the cost of the headhunter suddenly feels like a reasonable price to pay to have the right candidate commit to the job and start working ASAP.

Many headhunters *don't* usually interact with people who are actively looking for jobs and are likely to have already seen the company's posting. Instead, they are often embedded in a particular community of professionals and know who to approach about the possibility of leaving one job for another one. The incentive to change jobs may be for a promotion in title and/or pay, perhaps to leave an unsatisfying company, or perhaps to move on to more challenging work. Headhunters go to conferences, they ask people about their contacts in order to fill out their own network of connections, and they frequently cold-call to establish a broad base of possibilities when a company hires them to find a suitable candidate for a particular job. One headhunter estimated that headhunters as an industry fill only about 5 percent of the jobs available, and typically manage to help fill only about 20 percent of the jobs they are hired to fill. Clearly the work of a headhunter involves a difficult process but can potentially work to the advantage of all parties. Unfortunately, the use of a headhunter is also fraught with complications for you, the candidate, which we will outline in this chapter.

Before we get to the specifics of managing your relationship with a headhunter (and avoiding some of the possible pitfalls), let's walk through an analogous use of agents. Real estate agents, like headhunters, are agents in the sense that they negotiate on your behalf. In that case, they are the intermediary when you are buying or selling property. And real estate agents, unlike headhunters, are relatively common; they are vivid and relatable to most people. Thus, real estate agents are a good example to illustrate the basics of dealing with agents (and you might even learn a thing or two about real estate negotiations in the process).

The real estate market is set up to provide both buyers and sellers with a trained professional to help in the search, offer, and transaction processes. This trained professional is an intermediary (like the headhunter). There are pros and cons to this particular setup. First, the benefits: agents can do a number of things for us that (in theory) we either cannot do for ourselves or cannot do as readily as they can.

1. *Expertise*. Agents can provide content expertise about a particular geographic area. If you happen to be moving to a different state, a local real estate agent can often provide you with easy access to information about things like school districts, commuting options and time, community activities, etc.

2. *Distance*. Agents, as a third party, can allow for a greater degree of rational objectivity in the negotiation process. While the decision to bid on a house tends to be a very emotionally intense one for us, the agent has the advantage of being distanced from the emotional aspects of the deal and can keep a level head during the negotiation process. Having an extra person in the process can also run some positive interference during the negotiations, either to separate the emotions of the two parties or to potentially protect either from losing face.

3. *Experience*. Agents negotiate all the time, while we tend to negotiate for the big things like houses and jobs far less frequently. The actual content of how to engage in these important negotiations can be learned over time, but having an expert do the work for you can work to your advantage.

4. *Networks*. Agents work in this industry and engage in the buy/sell process all the time, while you, the principal, do not. Thus, the agent's connections and networks can pave the way for smooth interactions.

Agents in job situations (headhunters) have similar advantages to agents in the real estate setting.

1. *Expertise*. Headhunters tend to know more than you might about market rates for certain skill sets in that particular industry or even in a particular company. In fact, headhunters report that they typically have to instruct *both* the firm and the candidate about what market rates are paying for certain types of jobs, and keep both sides reasonable about what they should expect from the other. Not only may a headhunter know about potential jobs or a good fit even before an official job is posted, but they may also know about smaller firms that would not ordinarily hit your radar screen. They also often know particulars about specific companies or departments where most people are happy versus those with high turnover—all information that would be more difficult, if not impossible, to get on your own.

2. *Distance*. Headhunters can go to bat for you without your emotions or nerves getting in the way. If desired, headhunters can also preserve your confidentiality during the initial phases of a job search, which can be important if you are currently working and not ready to tell your employer that you are considering leaving. And not only can headhunters pass your resume along, they can "sell" you as the best fit for this particular opening and the one who should be snatched up while you are still available. Your agent is also your sales team in this case. Finally, headhunters can also lend legitimacy to very senior searches for both sides of the employment table. (Who doesn't sound more impressive when having an agent negotiate for them?)

3. *Experience*. Like the real estate agent, the headhunter has been involved in many more job negotiations than you probably have. They can also offer you broader career counseling and assist in polishing your resume, making sure that you include an appropriate amount of detail for the particular job you are pursuing. In fact, some headhunters are adept at helping you highlight and quantify your appropriate accomplishments and responsibilities (money,

people, and skills) so that they will jump out and grab the attention of your targeted employer.

4. *Networks*. Perhaps most importantly, headhunters often have inroads and established relationships with a variety of companies where it might be difficult for you to make these connections on your own. Because of this, your resume is likely to get a lot more attention coming from a headhunter than it would coming from you through HR. In addition, headhunters often know the individuals with whom you will be interviewing and can guide you on what the company is looking for in terms of skill set and fit. Many will have a pre-interview discussion with you and may be so direct as to suggest what to say and what not to say, and how to frame your skills to best match what the hiring manager is looking for. They may even suggest what types of questions you should ask and what to stay away from. (Keep in mind, though, that they may also be coaching the hiring manager on how to sell the position and make somebody like you excited about the job so that they can attract good talent as well).

THE DOWNSIDE TO AGENT USE

So far, the use of an agent like a headhunter sounds very positive, but agency also presents some potentially troublesome issues for the principal (the principal in this case is you, the job candidate). For one thing, the more people you add to a negotiation, the more likely the whole negotiation is to fail to reach an acceptable agreement, even when the agents do not get paid unless the deal goes through.[1] This generally happens because of the increased difficulties in coordinating and communicating effectively with three or four people instead of two. Even when deals do go through, there are two other sources of problems for you, which are (1) the potentially misaligned incentive structure between you and the agent, and (2) loss of your control over what gets said and how it is presented in the negotiation.

Misaligned Incentives

To address this issue, we return to the more commonplace real estate example. Real estate agents typically get paid a percentage of the selling price of the house. Based on this, the straight economic incentive structure is such that both agents (the buyer's agent and the seller's agent) are actually working for the seller, since the higher the selling price, the higher their commission (the more money they take home). In reality, though, there is an even greater (misaligned) incentive structure at work, and it is called "solution mindedness." This indicates the incredible desire agents have to arrive at a solution, any solution at all, as opposed to impasse, or the two sides walking away from each other without a deal. Agents do make more money with higher settling prices, but this must be balanced by the binary yes-no aspect to the situation, in which a deal results in a payout whereas having no deal results in nothing. Therefore, a deal, any deal—even one that is not in the best interest of their clients— serves the primary economic interest of all real estate agents.

Now let's examine this same misaligned incentive structure from the perspective of headhunters in job negotiations. Your (contingency-based) headhunter essentially operates under a similar economic incentive structure as the real estate agent. Sure, on the surface, it is true that the more money you get in the offer, the more your headhunter stands to gain in commission. However, the far greater risk is that one or both sides will decide that the other is not presenting a reasonable offer and will leave the table altogether. Remember that the headhunter's most important goal is first and foremost to make the deal happen and to get the placement. How much you get in the offer is a distant secondary concern.

Departing from the real estate model, headhunters also have a strong preference for keeping their client-firms happy, since this placement has ramifications beyond the money they make by way of a onetime commission. Their bigger payoff comes from creating (or continuing) a stream of successful placements within that firm and industry. The actual dollars that you make—for example, the difference between making $100,000 or $120,000—boils down to a small amount more for the agent in the near term, and very little difference in the long run. If the headhunter feels that the firm will not move past $100,000 or so, it might not be worth the risk of alienating the company by asking for more than that, even if it is potentially in your best interest. (Note that even career centers in universities can have this problem, since the lasting relationship with the recruiting firm, and thus a stream of ongoing placements, can supersede the needs of any one student.)

In addition, you as a candidate for a particular job may have interests beyond just base salary compensation, but these may not matter as much to the headhunter who is paid based primarily on this one element of the deal. This may play out during the back-and-forth concessions stage of a negotiation, when agents may encourage you to forego elements of the job package other than salary, based more on their own incentives than on yours. Finally, it is possible that different firms pay different fees to the headhunters, making them predisposed to push certain jobs over others onto their candidates, should there be more than one option available.

Loss of Control

The second major disadvantage to the use of an agent is losing control over what gets said and how. Once again, we will use the commonplace real estate agent as our learning example. Research shows us that selling prices are *lowest* when agents know only the range the sellers are willing to accept (including the least amount they would settle for) and *highest* when agents know only the buyers' range (including the absolute most they would be willing to pay before they pass on the house and keep looking).[2]

In other words, if you are looking to buy a property and tell your agent that you could spend up to $600,000 on a house but prefer to spend closer to $550,000, it turns out that your final purchase price will likely be closer to $600,000 than if you had said nothing at all. Similarly, if the sellers tell their agent that although they would like to get more, they will actually sell for anything over $500,000, it turns out that the sellers will, on average, end up with a lower price, closer to $500,000, than had the agent not been given this information. This illustrates both the solution mindedness of agents (they will tend to go for the "sure" deal that is to their economic advantage) and that the information you reveal to your agent does influence the outcome in negotiations. But, you may be thinking, this does not matter, because it is up to you to accept or reject any offer and thus, what difference does it make what the agent knows or doesn't know? Plenty, as it turns out.

Yet another useful piece of human psychology to understand is the fact that people are more comfortable delivering messages that they believe their audience wants to hear as opposed to messages that the audience does not want to hear.[3] In other words, people prefer to give good news instead of bad news. In fact, people are so influenced by this drive that they will actually, both consciously and unconsciously, change both the words and the delivery of what they are saying to suit their immediate audience. Couple this tendency to bend information to the audience's ear with an agent's most direct and pressing incentive to make sure the deal goes through, and we create a perfect storm in which an agent (your head-hunter) might not take as much care to protect your interests as you would like or as you would do if you had no intermediary. What follows is an example of a direct and blatant change of the message by a real estate agent that completely compromised the principal:

A TRUE STORY

On television, there are many shows that allow us to observe the house buying and selling process up close. On one such show, the buyers explained to their agent that they would really like to get the house for X, and so wanted to present that as their offer and see what happens. They also informed their agent that their budget exceeded X by a reasonable amount. The next scene showed the buyer's agent walking into the living room of the house in question with both the sellers and their own agent present. The buyer's agent walked in and said, "I have good news for you, we have an offer to make you! Now, the offer is for X, but I'd like to remind you that *this is just their opening offer*."

What has that agent done? What are the chances that the sellers would accept X for their house after being reminded that this was "just an opening offer"? Pretty close to zero, right? In short, the agent just sold her clients right down the proverbial river. The agent had information given to her in confidence. The agent did not directly violate their principal's trust and reveal the actual amount that the buyer would pay, but definitely signaled, or "tuned" her message, to increase the chances that the sellers would get an offer they felt good about in the next round, and one that she judged them more likely to want to accept.

The same mechanisms can, unfortunately, influence a job negotiation through an agent. If you tell your headhunter that you would like to get $120K and that is what you would like the firm to hear, but truly at the end of the day you would accept anything over $100K, you have given that agent the ability and power to signal to the employer that, even if $120K is presented as your asking price, it is not a firm figure. This is consistent with our earlier advice about keeping your bottom line figure to yourself for as long as possible (see chapter 3). That being said, many headhunters will strategically decide not to proceed with you without knowing your bottom line, and then it is again up to you to weigh the merits of proceeding with the opportunity and the power of keeping some of this information to yourself. In this situation, it certainly pays to reveal information only as needed and not to preemptively offer information that could potentially limit your amount of gain. Headhunters tend to know the range of salary that the company can offer, and want to know the same from you. They will likely ask you in turn: How much do you currently make? Would you leave for the same amount? How much more would it take for you to leave for another job? (In good economic times, people typically require 7–15 percent more to leave; in poor times, it can be as low as 4–7 percent).

TIP

If possible, do not reveal information to your headhunter about your "range" of acceptable numbers. Only proceed with one bid at a time.

Headhunters may even use an anchoring technique against you by strategically managing your negotiation goals and expectations. This is done by "beating" the candidate down before an offer is made by lowering their expectations about what they should expect to get paid. Thus, once an actual job offer comes through, the candidate will be thrilled with it. For example, if a headhunter knows that a job might pay between $110K and $115K, the candidate might be told that a reasonable offer for that type of position with that person's skill set and experience at this particular firm is between $100K and $105K, so that when the salary offer comes in higher than that, the candidate feels on top of the world and thinks the offer is too good to pass up. This is anchoring, this time being used to the agent's advantage (and to your disadvantage).

Misunderstandings

We have already discussed how an intermediary may strategically control the information you or your potential employer hears. But when you start adding people to the chain of communication, as when you negotiate through an agent, you also increase the odds for misunderstandings. Picture the children's game of "telephone," in which someone whispers a message to one person, who passes it on to the next, and the next, and by the time it reaches the last person in a chain, the message is invariably different, usually in quite substantive and often unexpected ways, from how it started. This game works because of unintentional misunderstandings in the communication of the message. Also remember that messages can get twisted intentionally if the agent feels that it might move the negotiations along. Information that is either unconsciously or intentionally changed, or omitted because it seemed risky or irrelevant to the intermediary, can lead to misunderstandings that may result in inefficient agreements, or worse, no agreement at all.

A TRUE STORY

Natalie was negotiating for a job through a headhunter, and the offer on the table from the firm was $10K lower than what she was prepared to accept. The HR representative from the firm wouldn't budge a bit on it. Finally, in exasperation, Natalie called the hiring manager directly and explained that she needed the money to help allay child care costs and could also work it out another way if she could have more flexibility in her work arrangement and a slightly better benefits package. The manager said, "I didn't know any of this. If I had known that earlier I could've helped out, but now I've given the offer to someone else and it has been accepted."

Having the headhunter and the HR representative understand her salary demands in this case was not enough; she actually needed to explain her needs and her willingness to trade some things off for others directly to the hiring manager, who clearly never got this message. Buyers and sellers in the real estate market typically do not have the opportunity to bypass their agents and speak directly with one another, and so most often choose to blindly trust the friendliest agent they can find in hopes that it will all work out. By contrast, you as a job candidate can have, and should have, your own channel of communication with the hiring managers in the firm.

Another strategy that agents like headhunters use on occasion is a hardball tactic known as "good cop, bad cop." This tactic relies on the psychology of intimidation and uses two teammates in different ways—one seems harsh and unreasonable, and the other seems kindly and accommodating but also has to bow to the wishes of the harsh one. Police detective shows on TV often demonstrate this tactic. During the interrogation of a subject, one cop gets angry and threatens the interviewee with harm (physical or legal, or both) if he or she does not tell them what they want to hear. Then the other, kinder cop dismisses the harsh one and says something to the effect of "I know he's unreasonable, I'm going to do my best to help you out here, but you need to give me something to work with." Car dealers also use this tactic but in a different way—by always having to go "in the back" and check with the manager about particulars of a deal, they are removing final authority from themselves and placing it with another, seemingly less reasonable, person. Any agent who has to "check with the folks upstairs" about an offer is using the same tactic.

Headhunters, like all agents, are prone to this dynamic because they can encourage each side to bend to the requirements of the deal based on the less-reasonable demands of the other side. This is only problematic if the agent dips into untruths to push one side or the other around. Consider the true case of the music agent who told the record company that the artist demanded perks such as first-class travel for herself and her staff. The company, sensing that the agent was being more demanding than the artist herself, requested a face-to-face meeting with the artist and was able to salvage the deal.[4]

TIP

Maintain a direct line of communication with the hiring manager if at all possible.

MANAGING YOUR HEADHUNTER RELATIONSHIP

As we have mentioned before, when you are in a job negotiation, you need to manage the process and relationships respectfully, and this same principle applies when negotiating through a third party like a headhunter. Only now you have even more relationships to manage. In addition to the hiring manager, you should also treat the headhunter respectfully. If you were to offend your headhunter, you risk creating a highly networked and potentially influential enemy in your industry. Headhunters can and do tell hiring managers negative things about candidates. In fact, because hiring someone is largely a process of elimination among qualified candidates, hiring managers tend to look for reasons to rule people out. Given this, even a hint of negative information from the headhunter is usually enough to get you crossed off the list for further consideration.

A TRUE STORY

Liam was pitched a position by a headhunter without initially being told which company had the job. Liam did a little research and figured out which company it was likely to be, and decided to apply for the position directly through the company instead of going through the headhunter. The headhunter, upon discovering this, called the hiring manager and said, "This guy's a liar; don't waste your time on him." Not only did Liam not get the interview, he was not likely to ever be considered by this firm again.

Let's look more specifically at proactive steps that will make your relationship with your agent run smoothly, and increase your odds of getting the maximum value out of that connection without falling into one of the many possible traps.

1. *Be honest and upfront about any problem situations or conditions.* Again, this does not mean that you have to reveal every thought or decision-point in your head, but it does mean that you should not mislead your agent. Agents cannot do their jobs effectively if they are working from misleading or mistaken information. Ask yourself if there is anything relevant to your situation that you need to tell your headhunter.

FOUR TRUE STORIES

One headhunter talked about a candidate who said he was willing to move and liked the new offer, but when the time came for an action from the candidate, he said he could not sell his house because it had lost so much value in the 2009 market crash that he was going to wait until it was worth more before moving.

Another headhunter tells of asking a candidate a dozen different times if he was engaged in any interviews with other firms, and was told no, only to have the candidate cancel the focal interview the day before it was scheduled because he took another job.

One told of a candidate who turned down a job because it did not provide the necessary flexibility for caring for an aging parent, about whom the headhunter knew nothing until it was too late.

One headhunter spoke of a candidate who lost a job opportunity because of the discovery of an old DWI charge that she had thought nobody would find out about and so she did not disclose it.

Our advice is that you should explain whatever problems or situations that you may have up front. Honesty also entails making sure that you act the same when you interact with the headhunter as with the firm. This agent needs to represent you and so needs to know what you are like. If you should turn down a job offer, then be honest with the headhunter about why. This can help the headhunter to potentially find a more suitable fit for you in another company.

2. *Be willing to wait.* As we described earlier, negotiations through multiple parties are usually slower than traditional one-on-one bargaining. However, if you know it is not going to work, don't waste your agent's time–go ahead and end it promptly.

A TRUE STORY

One headhunter told of a negotiation that dragged on for a full six months, and after all that work, the candidate ended up rejecting the offer, annoying the headhunter in the process.

3. *Know exactly what you want.* This is the time for crisp and concise communicated requirements. When you work with an agent, it is not the time for thinking out loud or exploring complex contingencies in your thought processes. Yet you must also be realistic about your worth. Prepare lots of information for your headhunter with respect to justifying your salary requests. If applicable, give your bonus history for at least the last three years in addition to your base pay, and give before and after figures in a poor economy (that is, what you were making before the economic decline and what you are making now).

4. As mentioned throughout this book, *be respectful.* In regard to headhunters, this also applies after they represent you. Too many times, headhunters tell us that candidates act like their best friend when they are searching for a job but then completely ignore them, or treat them badly in other ways, once they have the offer. Most professions tend to be networked. Since it is not impossible that you will be searching for new job opportunities again at some point in the future, it is wise to not burn any bridges.

A TRUE STORY

One headhunter mentioned a candidate who rejected an offer and never bothered to inform the headhunter of that decision. The headhunter swore never to represent this candidate again.

Similarly, don't badmouth anybody—many companies keep databases of their candidates, often going back several decades, and notes on this type of behavior can keep you on the outs. You want to manage your relationship and your impression with a headhunter the same way you would manage your relationship and impression with a hiring manager. Your headhunter will certainly ask you why you are potentially willing to leave your job, and if you whine about your current manager, it might reflect more poorly on you than it does on your current boss, even if the complaints are well deserved.

5. *Ask headhunters for lots of information.*
   a. First, ask for information about their data on current market rates for your skill set. They have this data, and you would be wise to take advantage of it to help benchmark, and justify, your requests during the negotiation. Remember, only you can decide what the right value is for you to accept a job, but gathering information can always help, and this is a ready source.
   b. Ask them for the scoop on working in a particular firm, or even potentially with a particular department/manager. Headhunters are busy watching people come in and out of the firms they deal with and often know if something is afoul someplace. You, in contrast, potentially do not have this type of information at your fingertips.
   c. Ask them what others have negotiated for in their employment package with a particular firm. As we discussed in chapter 1, sometimes salary structure is negotiable, and sometimes it is not. Sometimes job description is negotiable. Flexible working arrangements tend to be negotiated on a case-by-case basis, so you can find out if there is precedent in this firm for conditions like those to be included in a contract.

6. *Use your agent as a strategic filter.* For example, you probably would not share your medical history with a hiring manager in an interview, but you can allow your agent to put your requirements on the table as part of a larger package without getting bogged down in the details the way you might if you needed to discuss the situation yourself.

7. *Maintain relationships with one or more headhunters* in your industry over time and even when you are not job searching. It costs you nothing but can be an asset to your career path at some point even if you do not envision changing jobs immediately.

SUMMARY

The main goals of headhunters are to fill positions, to maximize their own payouts, and to satisfy the companies that they are recruiting for. Working with a headhunter can be a significant advantage for you, primarily because being presented to a firm at the headhunter's recommendation will get you more attention than applying on your own. Headhunters typically have more contacts and more information about a given industry than most job candidates, and you can take advantage of these benefits by carefully managing your relationship with the headhunter or executive search firm. If you were to remember only three things from this chapter about dealing with headhunters, it should be these:

- Be open and honest with the headhunter about most of your needs and any potential issues you may have with the job, but don't necessarily give away your bottom line.
- Keep an open line of communication with the hiring manager when possible.
- Remember that you need to focus on your own priorities because nobody else, including agents who have their own economic incentives to look after, is going to consider everything that you need or want as seriously as you will.

NOTES

1. Bazerman, M. H., et al., The effects of agents and mediators on negotiation outcomes. *Organizational Behavior and Human Decision Processes*, 53, 1992: 55–73.

2. Valley, K. L., et al., Agents as information brokers: The effects of information disclosure on negotiated outcomes. *Organizational Behavior and Human Decision Processes*, 51, 1992: 220–236.

3. Thompson, L., *Organizational behavior today*. Upper Saddle River, NJ: Pearson Prentice Hall, 2008.

4. Negotiation, decision-making and communication strategies that deliver results. In *Program on Negotiation at Harvard Law School Newsletter*. Harvard Business School Publishing, 2006.

EIGHT

Special Circumstances: Bad Economies, Family Businesses, and Cross-Cultural Negotiations

Context issues can complicate matters a great deal. In this chapter, we focus on three context variables that might relate to a job negotiation sometime in your career—or not. They are (1) the difference between good and poor economies for negotiating your job package, (2) family businesses, and (3) cross-cultural negotiations. Use these sections as needed.

SPECIAL CIRCUMSTANCE 1: STRATEGIES FOR POOR ECONOMIC TIMES

A popular belief is that during tough economic times, there is little room to negotiate within job contracts—this is, in reality, only a half-truth. On the one hand, it is true that there are typically fewer jobs to be had during an economic downturn, so the competition to get a job offer goes up. If, however, you happen to get a job offer or are currently employed during an economic slump, the chances are high that when it comes time to negotiate your employment package, you will put your negotiation skills to an even stronger test than usual. We tend to see the most creative and well-negotiated job packages during economic downturns. The reason is simple. The focus on base salary as the single and most important issue in the negotiation diminishes in this climate, allowing both parties (you and your employer) to focus more on the entire package. In tough economic times, knowing how to negotiate *well* can actually give you more of an edge over your peers than during good times. Put another way, in booming times, a bidding war for your talent and "wow" salary offers may well take care of much of the need for you to negotiate at all. This luxury does not usually exist in poorer economic climates, and so knowing how to negotiate well is even *more* critical in tough economic times when resources and opportunities become scarce.

FOUR STRATEGIES: ADDING/TRADING ISSUES, ANCHORING, JUSTIFYING, AND CONTINGENCY

Adding or Trading Issues

There is a temptation in a tough market not to negotiate at all, but to simply take whatever opportunity, or hardship, is handed out with an understanding that times are tough for everybody and you need to just play the cards you are dealt. Instead, we urge you to dig deeper into your toolbox of negotiating skills and focus more on thinking creatively, and outside the "base compensation box," to figure out what value you can deliver to the potential/current employer while still getting your own needs met. In other words, instead of focusing on "who gets how many dollars," the focus should rest even more squarely on the various types of opportunities and options available to both sides. This is often accomplished by bringing other issues to the negotiating table and possibly trading reduced salary in return for something else.

TWO TRUE STORIES

In the 2009 global economic crisis, the U.S. economy shed millions of jobs and unemployment rates approached 10 percent. During this time, Roger was informed he was going to be laid off from his firm because there was not enough work to keep him busy. Instead of going quietly, Roger analyzed his career goals and the resources available at his firm. He approached his managers with a new idea for his contract. He proposed that he would continue working in his current role to the extent that work was available for him to do, and any extra time he had was to be spent working on the company's charitable work to the community. Though his department's budget was being squeezed, the charitable arm of the company was, for the moment, in solid shape and could afford his slack time. Thus, his manager got to reduce his payroll bottom line and he got to successfully renegotiate his contract and keep his job. Furthermore, he found himself even more satisfied with his life, as he was able to devote some time to something he found especially meaningful.

Meanwhile, Dominic was working in finance when the economy tanked, and proposed to his manager that instead of being let go, he be permitted to take a two-year leave of absence without pay so that he could try out a career in teaching. The firm was so thrilled with this idea—not only did they save money, but they hopefully will have a skilled employee returning to them in better times without the pain of recruiting someone brand new—that they agreed to the leave and offered him a small discretionary account for teaching supplies. Dominic's previous years with his six-figure salary, coupled with the safety net of being able to return in a few years to his previous job in the financial industry, made the option of teaching for a little while into a reality instead of a back-of-his-head dream.

In both cases, Roger and Dominic added issues to the table (working for the charity arm of the company, and taking a leave, respectively, instead of being let go entirely) as well as offered trades (in both cases, the trade was current level of salary for other interesting work and opportunities, as well as the potential for a future return to the previous work). In both cases, they are likely to have saved themselves the professional and personal difficulties associated with being let go. Negotiation skills and creative exploration of the options turned both of these stories into happy endings. Remember, the value of the deal is the overall value to you, not just the dollars-and-cents value of the immediate package on the table.

Anchoring, or the First Mover Advantage

To put it as simply as possible: Go first. Earlier in the book, we described how much it changes people's thinking to have a number, or a proposal, already in front of them when they are doing their own estimates and making their own decisions on what to do. In tough economic times, it can be that much more valuable to preempt negative thinking ("We just don't have the budget to keep you on") with realistic options ("I am willing to move locations; I can do a slightly different job"), making that the new base from which future thinking expands. Too many decisions like employee cutbacks are made behind closed doors and before any discussion (or chance at negotiation to change the situation and the outcome) is permitted to happen. In this situation, you need to jump in and make your solution heard before ink gets put to paper, so to speak, on their decisions. How you accomplish this is by doing early and thorough research into the possibilities for the company, and for yourself and your time. Employers tend to be receptive to this kind of tactic, provided that it is framed in ways that address meeting *their* needs, and not just your own.

Whether negotiating or renegotiating a contract, Roger's example above demonstrates the value in understanding all of the assets, and the challenges, facing that particular firm. Are certain lines of business thriving or shrinking more than others in this economic climate? What about different areas of the country, or even different countries? What is on your list of career and life goals that might help to provide new options for the current conversation? Any of these lines of thought may help to unlock what seems to be a stalemate between your wanting what you might have gotten in better times and the company's looking only to save money off the bottom line. And, being ahead of the game in thinking along these lines and presenting options for yourself to your employer can put you in a position to set the agenda for a productive and successful negotiation.

A TRUE STORY

Brooke worked as a district manager for a chain of drug stores and was informed by her vice president that they were going to have to reduce the budget by 10 percent in the next fiscal year. Among the options on the table were store closings and layoffs. Brooke was concerned that the possibility of combining districts would result in too many district-level managers, and thus would threaten her job. She did some research by contacting other managers in other regions of the country, and found out that the area where she was originally from was actually expanding while the one she was currently working in was shrinking. Before other district managers could beat her to the punch, she approached her boss with an idea that would help to cut costs in her current region by combining districts, while helping the company grow in its booming market by transferring her to a place where there was still a need for people with her skills. The deal went through, and she was able to move internally in the company to a place she liked and helped her boss reduce his budget—a trade that allowed both sides to claim victory.

It seems worthy of some clarification here that this advice may feel different from chapter 3, where we extolled the wisdom of specifically *not* being the one who should speak first in a job negotiation, but to let the other side put the numbers on the table first. Let us clarify this. In this case, the kind of first-mover-advantage is *not* just being the one to say a high number first. In a bad economy, that could work against you in even more ways than the potential problems we covered earlier. Instead, in this chapter, we put forth the strategy of preemptively offering *solutions* to a situation that is likely to be faced with constraints. Here, you can put yourself in the other side's shoes by specifically asking/researching the areas where the constraints are going to be the most stringent, and then look for options that can work around that set of issues.

Justifying

Even more so than job negotiations in good economic times, justifying why what you are asking for is reasonable in a poor economy is paramount. While the old standards of previous salary, market rate, and others' salaries for the same work are still useful tools, justifying your requests specifically in terms of the value that you will bring/add/continue to provide for the company are the kinds of arguments that managers will need to use to justify their decisions to themselves and to those above them. Providing justification for your ideas requires you to first explain why you are making the proposal at all ("The company revenue is shrinking," "There doesn't seem to be enough work to keep everyone employed," etc.), and the benefits to the company of possibly doing things a different way ("You can reduce your annual budget," "You can use my talents in a new way," etc.), and then finally lay out why this plan makes sense for you personally ("I stay employed," "I get to do something I always wanted," etc.). While nothing guarantees acceptance, presenting your options in this way does increase the likelihood that your thoughts will be given serious consideration.

Contingency

Tight bottom lines increase the value of "if . . . then" types of arrangements. "If the company makes money, then I will get paid (but not otherwise)." Or, "If I perform above expectations, then I will get a raise." Contingent deals are a particularly good tool in your arsenal during poor economic times, but you don't want to place yourself in a position where you will end up without your actual goal, which is lucrative employment.

TWO TRUE STORIES

Ted had recently acquired his real estate license, and was hired at a commercial real estate firm just as the bubble was bursting in real estate. The company paid him a salary plus commission on the deals he helped out with. As the market went sour, so did the company's revenue, and they informed him that they didn't think they would be able to keep him. He approached the partners with the idea of paying him a staggered salary: If the company brought in $1 million of deals in the next six months, he would be paid at a certain rate; if the company brought in $5 million of sales, he would be paid a greater amount, plus he would still be able to keep his share of commissions on any deals he brokered. The company took him up on the offer. Unfortunately, the real estate bust was bigger than anybody expected, and he ended up working for free for six months before quitting.

On the other hand, Carolyn offered a similar deal to her sales manager by which instead of her current salary, she was able to negotiate a much larger percentage commission on accounts she brought in, in exchange for a smaller salary. She was able to work hard to make that financial arrangement at least neutral for herself for the time being and then it actually benefitted her once the economy picked up.

The key difference between the two is the scope of what was placed on contingency. In Ted's case, it was something too far outside his control, while in Carolyn's case, she was able to work hard and make the deal work for her. Contingency deals can work well to bypass an immediate shortfall of resources, but you want to make sure as much as possible that the desired outcome is within your reach.

NEGOTIATING FROM A POSITION OF UNEMPLOYMENT OR UNDEREMPLOYMENT

When you are unemployed or obviously underemployed for your skill set (such as if you take a job just to have some income because the right opportunity isn't yet available), it can feel daunting to know how to reset your salary to the industry norm again in the next opportunity you have for a job negotiation. It is a good idea to first remind yourself that when you negotiate with your potential employer, you are being hired to fill *that* job or position, and that is not based on your current (unemployed or underemployed) situation. The salary numbers you should focus on are the current typical market wages for the position you are filling. It helps to have some objective and explicit proof of the market wages for your particular skill set so your potential employer is not tempted to rely on your current salary (that is below the current market wage) for a benchmark. This means you need to do your research.

What should you do when they ask why you are unemployed or underemployed? There could be a number of reasonable responses for this. Were you let go as part of company-wide layoffs? Did you take time off for family reasons? Did you take a job as a temporary measure because you needed something immediately? Were you updating your skill set? The point is that you will want a very polished answer, complete with a good explanation, to cover why your current situation is what it is and reassure the potential hiring firm that your situation is reasonable and not based on something about your character. And after you explain it, move on. After the last two most recent economic downturns, being unemployed does not automatically hold the same stigma that it once did—sometimes it just means that although you are talented, you got caught in bad circumstances and are now available for immediate hire.

If, however, you have no good and reasonable explanation for being let go from your previous job (you were fired for cause, for example), you probably already recognize that you are in a position of tremendous weakness and may want to take any job you can get so that you can build your way back up to the kind of job you eventually want from a position of stability instead of unemployment with a questionable recent history. Attempting to hide this information is dangerous—it will probably turn up in background checks anyway, and then you have compromised your credibility as well as the potential for employment.

It is important to make sure you can present a reasonable case to explain your current situation due to the psychological tendency we all have to give *ourselves* a break while blaming *others* for negative situations. This is called the fundamental attribution error,[1] and to demonstrate it, we do the following exercise in our classes. We put students in pairs, with one playing the role of "salesperson" and the other playing the role of "supervisor." Those in the salesperson role are told that they are going to meet with their managers and need to explain why their performance has been poor over the last few weeks. Managers are simply told that their goal in the meeting is to understand the reasons for the salesperson's poor performance. Nobody is given any reasons for why the performance of this hypothetical salesperson has been bad—that's up to the individuals themselves to create and discuss.

A few interesting trends emerge. First, when students in the "salesperson" role were asked to list what kinds of reasons they offered for their poor performance, those reasons almost always fell along the lines of "the market was bad, competitors lowered their prices, you didn't give me enough training or a good product to sell" or even personal things like "I'm getting a divorce but the slip in my work won't happen again." Notably (and understandably), few if any people ever gave reasons along the lines of "I don't understand this new task" or "I'm just not that good at my job." Psychologists call this distinction the difference between external and internal attributions, or reasons that have nothing to do with me versus reasons that are all about me as a person. But although virtually all the salespeople gave reasons that amount to, essentially "It's not my fault—circumstances were such that this outcome would have happened to anyone," managers were still fairly likely to decide that the salespeople were actually either slacking off or not that capable. In other words, the excuses were often *not* taken at face value.

This translates into an attribution error whereby when you evaluate yourself, you tend to give yourself the benefit of considering the circumstances; but when you evaluate others, you tend to make attributions about the people themselves, without even intending to do so. For example, if you lie about something, you may explain that it was unavoidable, or only done to protect someone else's feelings, whereas someone else who lies is simply a liar. Your own outbursts of anger are explained by the miserable day you have had, or the poor treatment you have received, while someone else who does so is just a hothead. The tendency to do this is so universal that it is called the *fundamental* attribution error. You need to overcome this with a *convincing* explanation of why your situation is based on circumstance and not on your own shortcomings. Given their importance, there is no excuse for not preparing your comments on these types of topics ahead of time.

Lastly, a note from research may help you stay motivated in your job search. It probably comes as no great surprise that the intensity with which you engage in your job search predicts how quickly you will be reemployed, but it may not be as obvious that one of the most important predictors of how intensely you engage in the job search (along with how much financial hardship you are currently enduring) is how much you actually believe you *can* get a job.[2] It is crucial to actually believe that your efforts will pay off with employment.

POOR ECONOMIC TIMES SUMMARY

For those seeking jobs in tough economic times, the difficulty will be in landing a job offer as competition for open positions increases. Once you have an offer in hand, the principles of negotiation stay the same, but the need for effectively justifying the value that you will add to the firm—as immediately as possible—goes up, as well as the need to effectively explain gaps in your career path. And, you need to remember now more than ever that the focus should be on the overall package that you are receiving and not on any one issue (such as salary).

However, for those currently employed, the door is open for more complicated tradeoffs and renegotiations. Put yourself in the best possible situation in a troubled field or company via the use of effective negotiation tactics (adding/trading issues, anchoring, justifying, and using contingent deals). To do so, you should follow these four basic steps: (1) proactively *identify* the issues confronting your employer/boss, (2) be sure to *trade* issues—*adding issues* if necessary, (3) *anchor* the negotiation with *your* proposal, and (4) *justify* your anchor so they see the benefit to them as well as to you.

SPECIAL CIRCUMSTANCE 2: FAMILY BUSINESSES

Family businesses can have both tremendous assets and tremendous liabilities as a place to work. On the positive side, they are more nimble, more customer-oriented, more active in their communities, and even tend to outperform nonfamily firms on average.[3] They tend to have more free-flowing advice, expertise, and financial capital than a traditional firm.[4] If it is your own family's business, you also already know the "cast of characters," so to speak, and they know you. This means you can automatically skip some of the procedural aspects of normal interviews and job negotiations that nonfamily businesses have to go through. In addition, if trust already exists between members, this can enhance information sharing on the issues to be resolved. Finally, many family businesses were created as financial security for the family, and as such, the sense that you will be "taken care of" with respect to the financial aspects of your deal may be something you have the luxury of taking for granted. There is obvious attraction to such practices, but even these positive ties may not work in your best interest when it comes time to negotiating your job package. For example, considerable evidence suggests that when negotiators strive to protect their personal relationships (such as their friendships), they will not completely explore all negotiable options, leading to suboptimal deals.[5]

And unfortunately, all too many family businesses have problems unique to their circumstance. The rich history that exists between the family members can lead all parties to lose their perspective and professionalism, resulting in negative emotions and ineffective communication. Family relationships can become jeopardized in the course of office conflicts, making both work and home experiences unpleasant. The predominant conflicts can stem from issues of rivalry, guilt, and dependency.[6] Issues involving power such as responsibilities, authority, titles, and succession—all things that can come into play in job negotiations—are particularly sensitive areas in family business negotiations. In fact, while the majority of family-owned businesses are headed by someone older than age 55, fewer than 40 percent of them have a successor lined up, and less than half have either strategic plans or executives with the experience and qualifications typically seen in those roles.[7] Family businesses are predominantly run by a single decision-maker,[8] whose personal identity is often interwoven with the company as a whole,[9] making all decisions (and negotiations) more intense and more personal than they would be with a nonfamily manager. In fact, one scholar characterized the traditional owner of a family business as someone who "has great difficulty delegating authority" and "also refuses to retire despite repeated promises to do so."[10]

In either case, job negotiations amongst family members adds extra layers of complexity as a great deal of history typically exists between family members, and it is crucial to consider the (hidden) emotional and relational issues that are present while still keeping your objective interests in sight. There are also some unique issues that probably need to be addressed in this setting that differ from a more traditional job negotiation. Below is a list of suggestions for tackling a job negotiation in this particular setting.

1. *If conflict is likely, bring in someone else.* If you feel that direct one-on-one conversation is likely to be too emotionally charged to be productive, you might want to head it off at the pass and have someone else help to deflect the conflict away from you. Having another person present in negotiations helps to keep the emotions in check.[11] This can be done by having a neutral third person (already in the

business) sit in on the negotiations with you, having a third person to act as a mediator of sorts, or by asking another family member to act as an "agent" to negotiate on your behalf. Just make sure if you use this last strategy that you trust the other person and are very clear ahead of time with what you hope to accomplish and what are and are not acceptable outcomes for you. When all else fails, you have the option of bringing in outside help. One adult child of a family business stated that "if I could do only one thing differently, it would be to bring in someone from the outside at the beginning of my tenure here to help us set things up in a better way."

2. *Remember to negotiate every aspect of the job that you possibly can, not just the compensation element.* If there is one theme song that gets played again and again by people in family businesses, it is that tensions arise because the lines of responsibility are not clearly drawn. Experts say that it is critical to divide the tasks not just along the lines of who can accomplish what, but also to make sure that each employee has the chance to acquire and demonstrate competence and work in a complementary way with each other.[12] Similarly, having a very clear sense in your initial contract of how you will be appraised and on what you will be rewarded can be even more important in a family business setting.

TWO TRUE STORIES

Ellen and her husband, Jim, took their management degrees home to work for her father in the family's business, with the stated intent of having them take over the business slowly over time. They felt well cared for in terms of the financial packages and perks they were offered (company cars and the like), and were able to get hands-on experience and impressive job titles long before they would have been eligible for these same things at a traditional firm. Unfortunately, it was a disaster. Ellen says: "It was never clear which decisions were mine and which my father would come in with the final say. Even the other nonfamily employees were caught up in this and would ask me if I was sure about a decision or would my father come in and change it?" Even after she was made CEO of the company, her father couldn't really let go completely and would disappear and come in full of authority at seemingly random intervals.

On the other hand, brothers Benjamin and Daniel ran a successful business, which they attributed in part to the clean separation of responsibilities. Benjamin says: "I frequently had to tell employees that a particular issue was something that was the responsibility of my brother, and that they should go to him with the question." That separation helped them to remain partners and friends throughout their years of co-ownership.

In addition to responsibility, planning for the growth of the firm, and contingencies in place for poorer economic times can become hot-button issues if they are not clearly delineated at the beginning.

A TRUE STORY

Josh and his parents thought they had done a good job with succession planning and had made arrangements for him to take over his family's business when it grew to a certain size. Nobody had thought to plan for what happened if the business *didn't* grow, though, or didn't grow at a reasonable pace. Sure enough, the economy turned and lots of the business's clients fell on hard times. While the business survived, it failed to grow at anything like the predicted pace, and so the succession plan and buyout were put on indefinite hold, much to Josh's frustration. Furthermore, Josh's parents continued to consider the company to be their own and to take money from it as they needed to maintain their lifestyle, arguing that their fixed costs had not changed just because the business was bringing in less revenue. "If I had it to do over again," Josh later agonized, "I would absolutely have put a cap on the percentage of revenue that could be taken out by them, and would have been more complete in the plans for succession."

3. *I'm not a family member, but I'm negotiating with a family business.* Proceed with caution. Now more than ever, you need to talk to everyone you can inside the firm and find out what it is really like, what kinds of tensions might exist, and whether outsiders are truly given a chance at promotion even without the family name behind them. While some family businesses can be warm and wonderful places to work, you do not want to find yourself in the middle of a

dysfunctional family situation in need of therapy as opposed to professional expertise.

4. *Use contingency deals.* Family situations can often benefit from "if . . . then" deals because it makes the required outcomes for reward more tangible. For example, perhaps you want a particular title or salary that the business is reluctant to bestow upon you. Family businesses tend to be more open to a deal structured along the lines of "if I deliver X amount of business in my first year, then I will get paid Y and will become a vice president." Although such contingency deals work in any job negotiation, family businesses are often even more open to such a structure.

FAMILY BUSINESS SUMMARY

Negotiating job contracts in a family business are typically more complicated than standard offers from nonfamily firms. While many of the principles in this book still apply, you must also now take into account the relational history as well and understand that ill-defined work processes, authority, and succession plans are the bane of many a family employee. Use the advantages to your favor (trust and insider information), and take steps to avoid the hazards by using third parties to help avoid family tensions, and by being all the more explicit about exactly what your job is and is not, how and when you will be rewarded or promoted, and what to do when things go awry.

SPECIAL CIRCUMSTANCE 3: CROSS-CULTURAL NEGOTIATIONS

Cross-cultural negotiations result in agreements of lesser value than within-culture negotiations, on average.[13] This is in no small part because of the basic differences in what we are trained to expect from the process of negotiations. For example, when we say the word "negotiation" to you, does it imply a scenario in which you are going to communicate directly with another party or parties to work out a possible arrangement, or does it imply that you will most likely seek an intermediary to present your case to someone else? Does a 1:00 p.m. meeting mean that the meeting will start at 1:00 p.m. sharp, or that 1:15 is fine too, or that people will wander in around 2:30 p.m. or later? The answers may well depend on what country you are in. Different national cultures can give rise to different assumptions about the fundamental ways in which we should communicate, interact, and problem-solve. Dealing with an international negotiation can change the game significantly. While this book is not the place for a detailed look at what to expect from each different culture that you may encounter, it may be useful to understand some guiding principles about what changes when negotiations take on an international dimension.

First and most importantly, we need to clear the air on the generalizations that we are about to present. For one thing, it can be difficult to talk about the single culture of a large group—for example, are people from New York, Texas, and Los Angeles all part of the same culture? For another, when you are slated to meet with an individual, you actually have no way of knowing whether that one person will conform to the cultural standards that you expect. In other words, though you are planning to meet with a Japanese businessman and have prepared for what to expect in that case, you may find someone who is wholly comfortable with a more typically American style of business. People are unpredictable as individuals, but as groups we can talk about the *general tendencies* of what to expect. You prepare for the "average" but need to understand that you may well be interacting with someone who does not fit that mold. Do you feel like the "average" American (or whatever nation you are from), for example? So of course remember that someone you don't know is just that—a person full of traits yet to be discovered. Lastly, the situation in which people find themselves can also be powerful drivers of behavior.

DOES CULTURE MATTER?

Imagine you are dealing with a Chinese company to work in a department based in Chicago, headed by a German, and you are Canadian. Does culture matter? Yes, but it is largely dependent on what culture is triggered for that particular interaction.[14] Each of us, as individuals, is often made up of several different aspects to our identity. For example, our "professional" selves may act one way, while our "at home with the family" selves might act quite differently. Similarly, even within a national culture, there may be different possibilities for how we can expect others to act. The point for you is that understanding the context may help you sort out what is considered appropriate behavior for any one situation.

A TRUE STORY

Casey, a soon-to-be-minted MBA, interviewed for a job with a Japanese company. The company had organized a social event, a barbecue, at a

local hotel for all of the candidates who were scheduled to be interviewed the following day. Casey prepared for the event by learning
about the company and Japanese customs. At the reception, he was
greeted by a company representative, and when Casey handed him his
business card along with a Japanese-inspired bow, the company
representative responded, "Have a beer, man, and save that crap for
somebody else."

When you are in doubt, watch the behavior of others if possible for
clues as to what is appropriate in the given situation. Hence, when dealing
with cross-cultural job negotiations, be aware of what environmental triggers are at play. Is it a business professional setting? Are you meeting at
an ethnically rich event? What is everybody else doing?

A CLOSER LOOK AT SPECIFIC CULTURAL DIVIDES

The most defining divide in terms of cross-cultural differences is East
and West. As opposed to Eastern cultures, Western cultures tend to be:

1. More focused on advancing the individual self as opposed to looking out for the whole group (a distinction called individualism versus collectivism).
2. More verbally direct in their search for information and their
   approach to discussions (called Low Context as opposed to High
   Context, since in High Context cultures, much of the relationship
   tends to be understood by both sides based on hierarchy or network
   cues without the need for much discussion).
3. More equal in the opportunity afforded to anyone to acquire power, as
   opposed to having strict social strata that are hard, if not impossible, to
   alter (called egalitarian cultures, as opposed to hierarchical cultures).[15]

Taken together, these traits help describe Westerners as negotiators who are:

1. More comfortable getting straight to the point in a negotiation as
   opposed to spending significant amounts of time first developing
   the relationship as might be important to many Eastern cultures.[16]
   Westerners exchange information more directly[17] but are less comfortable inferring each other's priorities by exchanging many offers
   in succession.[18]

2. More concerned with their own outcome than the interests of the other side.

3. More likely to seek outside opportunities to improve their negotiating positions.

Due to these behaviors, Westerners become vulnerable to coming across as aggressive, impersonal, and overly intense.[19] Western cultures tend to value and reward those who "stand out" from their peers by highlighting their positive traits, while Eastern cultures look for those who "blend in" with their group by focusing more on their negative traits[20] and by demonstrating humility, deference, and respect.[21] Again, the only conclusion to draw from this sampling of potential areas of miscommunication and misinterpretation is that you need to learn as much as you can about what to expect ahead of time, talk to someone who knows the culture well, and then watch the situation for cues as to how to proceed effectively.

THE LANGUAGE BARRIER

The use of English as a global language in business is becoming widespread, but if you are dealing with an international company, you may find yourself in a job negotiation with someone who speaks a language different from your own. This type of situation brings in additional issues to deal with in job negotiations.

Use a foreign language only if you already speak that language extremely well. Otherwise, you risk misunderstandings, or the possibility that your focus on the technical aspects of speaking correctly will replace your ability to focus on the details of negotiation itself, which is a full-time job as it is. If you must negotiate in a language that is not your native tongue, then you might want to consider using a translator or interpreter. Doing so will alter the dynamics of the negotiation, and you should be prepared for how to approach this situation. Two tips in particular can help lessen the burden of using a translator.[22] First, practice with a translator. Using a translator alters the pace of dialogue and requires you to speak in shorter chunks versus long narratives. In addition, you will also want to speak at a slow pace to allow the translator to more accurately capture what you are saying. Second, if possible, consider bringing your own translator and brief this person ahead of time on the details of what you expect to be discussed and what you hope to convey. Even if you are not able to use your own translator, you might request a preparatory conversation with the translator before you begin the session so that you two can get comfortable with one another, and so that your speaking style won't be new to the translator during the negotiation itself.

Lastly, we'd like to comment on international assignments, which of course place the culture issue even more front-and-center since your whole life will suddenly become an experience in cross-cultural interactions. In terms of the job negotiation specifically, in this situation it is critical to learn not only about the norms of interaction in the other culture, but also about the employment laws. These may differ significantly from what you are used to, and a knowledgeable employee is the one who stands the best chance of taking advantage of the various options.

A TRUE STORY

Scott worked for a U.S. firm in London for long enough that he was eligible for establishing residency there and requested that he become treated as an EU employee (with an EU contract) instead of a U.S. one. When it came time for Scott and his wife to adopt a baby, this difference had significant implications as EU employees were entitled to 30 days' paid leave for adoption and U.S. employees were not. In fact, his manager forgot that he was on an EU contract and decided to terminate him when he said he was going out on leave, only to find out that his EU contract prevented that from happening.

CROSS-CULTURAL NEGOTIATIONS SUMMARY

Overall, the universal culture of business is emerging such that people globally are becoming more comfortable with the same ways of doing things over time. Yet real differences still exist, and being as prepared as possible for them is the only effective way to go.

NOTES

1. Ross, L., The intuitive psychologist and his shortcomings: Distortions in the attribution process. In *Advances in Experimental Social Psychology*, L. Berkowitz, Editor, 173–220. Orlando, FL: Academic Press, 1977.

2. Wanberg, C. R., R. Kanfer, and M. Rotundo, Unemployed individuals: Motives, job-search competencies, and job-search constraints as

predictors or job seeking and reemployment. *Journal of Applied Psychology*, 84, 1999: 897–910.

3. Ibrahim, N. A., J. P. Angelidis, and F. Parsa, Strategic management of family businesses: Current findings and directions for future research. *International Journal of Management*, 25, 2008: 95–110.

4. Sorenson, R. L., and L. Bierman, Family capital, family business, and free enterprise. *Family Business Review*, 22, 2009: 193–195.

5. Fry, W. R., I. J. Firestone, and D. L. Williams, Negotiation process and outcome of stranger dyads and dating couples: Do lovers lose? *Basic and Applied Social Psychology*, 4, 1983: 1–16.

6. Levinson, H., Conflicts that plague family businesses. *Harvard Business Review*, 1971.

7. Simmonds, R., The family business: Failing to plan is commonplace. *Financial Executive*, 23, 2007: 20.

8. Feltham, T. S., G. Feltham, and J. J. Barnett, The dependence of family businesses on a single decision-maker. *Journal of Small Business Management*, 43, 2005: 1–15.

9. Milton, L. P., Unleashing the relationship power of family firms: Identity confirmation as a catalyst for performance. *Entrepreneurship: Theory and Practice*, 32, 2008: 1063–1081.

10. Levinson, Conflicts that plague family businesses.

11. Coltri, L. S., *Alternative dispute resolution: A conflict diagnosis approach*. Upper Saddle River, NJ: Pearson Prentice Hall, 2004.

12. Levinson, Conflicts that plague family businesses.

13. Brett, J. M., and T. Okumura, Inter- and intracultural negotiation: US and Japanese negotiators. *Academy of Management Journal*, 41, 1998: 495–510.

14. Fu, J., et al., Spontaneous inferences from cultural cues: Varying responses of cultural insiders and outsiders. *Journal of Cross-Cultural Psychology*, 38, 2007: 58–75.

15. Brett, J. M., Culture and negotiation. *International Journal of Psychology*, 35, 2000: 97–104.

16. Zhu, Y., B. McKenna, and S. Zhu, Negotiating with Chinese: Success of first meetings is the key. *Cross Cultural Management*, 14, 2007: 354–364.

17. Adair, W. L., T. Okumura, and J. M. Brett, Negotiation behaviors when cultures collide: The U.S. and Japan. *Journal of Applied Psychology*, 86(3), 2001: 371–385.

18. Adair, W. L., L. Weingart, and J. Brett, The timing and function of offers in U.S. and Japanese negotiations. *Journal of Applied Psychology*, 92, 2007: 1056–1068.

19. Graham, J. L. and M. N. Lam, The Chinese negotiation. *Harvard Business Review*, 81, 2003: 82–91.

20. Heine, S. J., et al., Is there a universal need for positive self-regard? *Psychological Review*, 106, 1999: 766–794.

21. Kopelman, S., and A. S. Rosette, Cultural variation in response to strategic emotions in negotiations. *Group Decision and Negotiation*, 17, 2008: 65–77.

22. Salacuse, J., *The global negotiator: Making, managing, and mending deals around the world in the twenty-first century*. New York: Palgrave Macmillan, 2003.

NINE

After the Deal: What's Next?

In this chapter, we address five common situations that may arise *after* you have successfully negotiated a job package. First, we discuss the situation in which you are underpaid relative to the market and would like to obtain a salary increase from your current employer, without damaging the relationship. Second, we discuss a similar situation in which you may have just improved your skill set by getting an advanced degree, or certification of some sort. Third, we discuss how to pave the road for future successful job negotiations (at this or another firm). Finally, in the fourth and fifth situations, we discuss the unpleasant situations in which the employing organization either backs out or does not fulfill their end of the contract after the deal is done.

SITUATION 1: RAISES

I'm underpaid. How do I negotiate a salary increase from my current employer?

This is one of the most common and toughest job negotiation situations. Let's assume that you want to stay with your company, but with a higher salary. As with so many areas of job negotiations, to make such a request, you need to present a reasonable justification for why you deserve more than you are already getting. This is usually done through a combination of two elements. First, you will need to highlight the value that you add to the company through your past accomplishments, and then you will need to signal your market worth. Presenting the value of your contributions and your accomplishments should be the easy part. Demonstrating your market worth without alienating the trust of your current employer can be trickier.

One of the most popular strategies that people use in trying to justify an increase in pay is to get an offer of employment elsewhere and then ask the current employer for a comparable salary. This tactic is often accompanied by a threat (either explicitly stated or just implied) of leaving the company for greener pastures if a salary increase is not forthcoming. This strategy is tempting and can be effective; however, we only recommend it *if you are truly prepared to take that other offer*. We offer instead a safer two-step variation of this tactic if your primary goal is to remain in your current job.

The first step is to understand the current financial situation in your company. In particular, explore whether or not your organization has the financial resources for providing raises and other perks at this time. This can typically be determined either through public records or through informal conversations with others in the firm. If they do not have the means for giving raises at the present time, you might elect to save the conversation for later. If they do, then you can move on to step two.

The second step is to realize what the norms are where you work. Norms, in contrast to evaluating your company's financial health, may be harder to grasp as they are not explicitly recorded. Instead, company norms are implicitly understood and learned over time and through repeated experiences. Although there are many norms that guide behavior in organizations, the one you are most interested in will be whether it is acceptable in your company to find other job offers and bring them back to your employer as justification for a pay increase. In many firms and industries, this is a perfectly acceptable practice, while in others, looking for employment at another company is viewed along the lines of treachery, and doing so will close off future doors of opportunity. You will learn your workplace norms over the course of time, but if you are unsure, ask some trusted colleagues for their opinion. If several people agree on the norm, then it is probably accurate. If you cannot get consensus, perhaps there is no universal norm on this matter, and each manager might react differently to the situation.

If you are in a firm or industry in which outside competitive offers are viewed as part of doing business, then finding a competing offer is usually the best tactic. In fact, some industries have moved to a system in which promotions and raises typically happen only by jumping ship to a competitor for a raise and promotion, and then coming back to your original firm at the higher level, sometimes in as little as a few months' time.

A TRUE STORY

Samantha and Karen were both managers at a consulting firm. Samantha got wooed away by a competitor for a 20 percent salary hike and a promotion to senior manager, while Karen stayed at her current job and continued to do excellent work. Six months down the road, the original firm re-recruited Samantha at what was now a 30 percent salary increase over her original salary and her new higher title. Karen realized that loyalty was not valued at her firm and began to look elsewhere for employment.

In this situation, go ahead and find out what the market wage is for your skill set by getting other offers. If these alternative offers happen to be above what you are currently making, then you can approach your current employer and respectfully point out that you are underpaid relative to your market worth. This approach is not without risk, however. If you do not have a track record of outstanding performance, your employer may very well suggest you follow through with the other offer. But if you do have a successful record, objective evidence of your market rate can be strong justification for a raise at your current job.

A TRUE STORY

Jonah wanted an out-of-cycle raise, but was told that the company never does that without a competing offer from an outside firm, which they needed to see in writing. So, Jonah went on the hunt, and received a tempting offer located in another part of the country. He ended up staying and getting his raise, but noted to his boss that the company gambled when they asked him to go out and get wooed by another firm!

When informing your employer about the alternative offer, be sure that you are explicitly clear in mentioning that your preference is to stay with the company and you simply would like them to reevaluate your current salary. State that you are bringing this offer to their attention because you feel your current compensation level is not up to industry standards. In this case, you should be the one to anchor the negotiation by explicitly letting them know exactly what you would like (a specific dollar amount, title change, or anything else) by using the other offer as justification. If you have any intention of actually staying on good terms at this firm, *do not* threaten your employer by saying you will quit and take the other offer if they refuse. Threats run the risk of entrenching people into their current positions, and instead you want them to amicably change the status quo. Be very respectful. In addition, be sure to remind them about your successful record and what they can expect from you going forward, such as continued high levels of performance.

As a side note, there is an ethical dimension to consider when exploring other offers that you have no intention of taking. On one hand, this strategy can be viewed as being unethical in that it expends the time, energy, and money of the hiring organization, when you have no intention of ever taking the offer if it should be extended. On the other hand, such tactics can be viewed as the norm for professional managers, and many professionals always seem to be exploring new opportunities. From this mindset, shopping around for job opportunities is simply the cost of doing business in a competitive marketplace where talent is necessary for success. In most industries, it is a perfectly acceptable practice, but you need to remain attuned to what feels comfortable and appropriate for your own situation.

A TRUE STORY

Jeanne was up for a promotion at her current job, and was told that there were some advocates for her case and some others that were working against her behind the scenes. A trusted senior-level manager told her in confidence that what she needed to do was to go out and get another offer from a competitor to help "seal the deal" for the promotion at her current job. The senior manager also noted that this was common practice in the industry and the other firm would understand when she did not end up taking the job—that it happened all the time. Jeanne put out feelers, and instantly got a strong nibble from another company about two hours away from her home. The job would have required some retooling for her, and for that reason in addition to concerns about uprooting her family, Jeanne was reluctant to take this offer. The new firm specifically asked Jeanne how likely she was to take the position and implied that they did not want to tie up the position by making her a formal offer if she was not likely to accept it. Even though in her industry it was acceptable practice to solicit and then turn down offers in order to get internal promotions, Jeanne just did not feel comfortable with making the second company issue her an offer given the low chances of her accepting it. She withdrew her application, and told her current firm, "I've received tremendous interest from Firm 2, but I withdrew my application to wait and see what you decide first, since my first choice is to stay here. You and I both know I could get another job, but I don't feel comfortable going that route—instead, you have the right of first refusal on me. Promote me and I'll stay, otherwise I'll be working for someone else." They promoted her.

On the other side, what do you do if the norm at your company is such that looking around for other opportunities is a sign of disloyalty? Unfortunately, in that case you have two further options, but both have some drawbacks. The first is to demonstrate that you know the market is paying more than you are earning *without* an actual other offer in hand. Comments like "I've been hearing from colleagues in the industry that others with my skill set/my title are making as much as 20 percent more than I am. I'm happy here and don't want to leave. I have helped X and Y projects come to successful completion in the past 12 months. I would like to raise the topic of my salary with you." This may not lead to the raise you are hoping for, but it is a reasonable way to broach the topic in this situation.

The other option for earning more is effective but also potentially more disruptive to your life. This is to actually leave your present employer for another company. In other words, go ahead and get another job offer, but do so with the intention of taking it. This can be the only way to reset your salary to the market level in some cases. That said, sometimes people choose to pass up the resetting of their salary because they enjoy the benefits of their current position, which might include higher seniority or greater vacation privileges, or because they are happier in their current geographic location and/or are balancing the needs of a dual-career family. Plenty of people may not earn the optimal salary possible because of these types of trade-offs. This is a conscious personal choice on your part and does not mean that you are acting irrationally, only that you are prioritizing something besides base salary. But economically speaking, if you find yourself in a company where the norms are such that looking for another offer is frowned upon, then the best strategy to get a higher salary may simply be to switch companies.

TIP

Asking for a raise is a threefold process. Make sure you (1) reassure your manager that you want to stay, (2) remind your manager of your accomplishments, and (3) signal your market worth through either direct (competing offer) or indirect (market data) mechanisms.

SITUATION 2: ADVANCED DEGREES AND CERTIFICATIONS

I just got a new degree/certification. How do I negotiate a salary increase to recognize this accomplishment?

Unfortunately, and much to people's surprise, a new degree or other qualification does not usually translate immediately into more dollars for the same work you were already doing before the extra qualifications. Instead, it merely makes you look more attractive for other positions you may eventually want to be considered for if and when you switch jobs. If you are currently employed and are embarking on a new certification or higher degree, the best thing you can do is to talk to your boss beforehand. Doing so can set an anchor for future discussions about salary or new job opportunities, so you may want to discuss the impact this may have on your future salary increases now, before actually doing the work or investing your personal time and money. Be sure to also talk about future reassignments before starting down such a path.

As a side note, one of the greatest job-related benefits of getting advanced degrees or certifications is from networking with like-minded peers who may know of better opportunities elsewhere. Finding an opportunity is directly related to the network you are embedded within. It seems that almost every academic year in our graduate-level classes, somebody ends up switching jobs due to a contact made in class. Furthermore, it is typically not the immediate contact who has the opportunity, but a classmate who knows of somebody who is hiring. This is known as the strength of weak ties (versus direct ties or people you already know personally).[1]

TIP

Do your best to know ahead of time what advanced training or degrees will earn you in the marketplace.

SITUATION 3: THE NEXT JOB NEGOTIATION

How do I best set the stage for my future job-related negotiation?

Though the primary purpose of this book is to obtain a successfully negotiated employment contract, we feel it would be a great disservice if we implied that this was the actual end of the job negotiation journey. Most professionals will likely have to renegotiate their employment terms at some point, whether it is during an annual performance review, a chance for promotion, or a new opportunity elsewhere either inside their current organization or from the outside. Whatever the reason, now that you have secured employment and signed the contract, it is time to begin effectively laying the groundwork for the next job negotiation. This is true even if you have no idea right now what that future role or job will be. To best take advantage of the *next* job negotiation opportunity, don't wait until that time is upon you, but do the prework *now* for the anticipated future (the prework is described in detail below). Doing this prework will make future job negotiations easier and, if done correctly, may even offer you more opportunities to realize than if you simply do your job, even if you do your job very well. Hard work and good outcomes alone will not necessarily carry you toward the next job assignment or hierarchical level. In addition to solid performance, your efforts in this regard would be wisely spent working on developing and managing the relationships in your job, particularly in the first year. Four specific tasks follow that may help you manage this process more effectively.

1. Set Up an Informal Meeting Periodically with Your Immediate Supervisor

An open line of communication about your current job performance, the status of the position you currently hold, and future opportunities can help keep you in the loop on important work to be done. It also shows your eagerness to do the best job that you can. While this may sound obvious, by far the vast majority of employees at all levels wait until their formal annual performance review to discuss these things. Waiting for the annual performance review is certainly the easiest option as it is built into most organizational systems, but it is less than ideal as a means of communication about one's future career path. For one thing, the formal and permanent nature of the feedback given annually heightens the tension for both sides. Annual reviews are typically among a manager's *least*-preferred activities of the year (not to mention among the most stressful for the employee). With emotions running high on both sides, effective information exchange drops to a very low level. Second, these reviews are often tied to bonuses or raises, making them more about a "number" and less about the work itself. Instead, you should remember that although the annual performance review is required by your company in part to ensure that managers keep track of the skills, accomplishments, and goals of their employees, in reality it offers little opportunity to distinguish yourself from others within the mounds of paperwork that are typically involved in this process. In addition, the once-a-year nature of most performance reviews is too infrequent to be of much strategic benefit to you in your job. In essence, the quality of communication in an annual performance review is inadequate to nurture the relationship you have with more senior leaders.

Given this, aim for something like a monthly meeting with your immediate manager to informally discuss your current projects, performance, and also get some indication of what will be next. Other items are likely to creep into the discussion as time goes by, including insights into where the company is headed and the potential for new opportunities. In addition, your immediate boss will more likely have you in mind when opportunities arise to be assigned, and to remember your hard work when the topic of raises eventually comes up. In summary, do not rely on the *formal* annual performance review to discuss your status and potential opportunities. Instead, rely on regular *informal* discussions with your immediate manager to keep a nurturing line of communication open and to set the stage for future job negotiations.

2. Get and Stay Involved in Both Social and Professional Realms

One of the unfortunate aspects about being the new hire is that you are placed into a collection of people who already have a history together and know how things work formally and informally at the company, while you are a stranger to them, as they are to you. The burden is on you to get involved and get to know as many people as you can. Of course, everyone will probably be friendly to you, and many will introduce themselves with the "standard" offer to contact them if you should be in need of any help. However, you should be the one to take the next step and make a more substantive connection. Ask people to lunch or coffee one at a time. Do not limit yourself to your peers, but connect with the full range of people around you—teammates, superiors, subordinates, and support staff. Go to all the events (company picnics and informal get-togethers) that you can. Doing so will send a clear signal that you are truly a part of the company, that you are accepting of its implicit and explicit norms, and people will start to notice you for your involvement and commitment to this company.

Second, be proactively involved professionally. The people who tend to be both noticed and successful are the ones who are viewed as going the extra mile professionally. To do this most effectively, actively seek the work you want to do. Instead of waiting for your tasks and goals to be given to you by your immediate supervisor (or laterally from your teammates), search for and request appropriate responsibilities. This includes being willing to ask about other projects and your possible involvement in them. Keep abreast and involved in what others are doing around you, and inform them of what you are doing. In other words, recognize who is accomplishing what and also make sure you let others know about your (positive) accomplishments. To be fair and politically generous, make sure your subordinates are recognized for their work. Often this entails merely updating superiors about the status and/or results of your work and those of your team and/or subordinates. Taking these steps will keep the notion that you are professionally involved and can deliver results in the forefront of those around you, including your superiors. Remember, lots of people do good work that goes unnoticed. Don't be one of them, and your next round of job negotiations will be all the easier.

3. Know Your Subordinates and Lateral Colleagues

Your subordinates and colleagues can either support or undermine your career path. These people are critical to your success, but are often taken for granted by new employees. Respect is never automatically forthcoming, regardless of your new title. Your peers comprise the network of people on whom you will need to rely repeatedly.

With subordinates, make sure you explicitly tell them about your role and what is expected of you by your own manager in addition to what you expect of them and what they can expect from you. These are all very important issues for them, especially at the beginning. Give as much priority to nurturing these relationships as you do with your superiors. This includes, but is not limited to, calling each person by name even if there are a lot of names to learn. One of the most successful professors at a top business school won accolades teaching a rather boring subject in no small part because he was able to learn and use the names of each and every one of his students. The students were impressed that he would take the extra time for them, and felt personally attended to, and the professor's popularity helped vault his career into the upper levels of the school's administration.

4. Keep Meticulous Records of Your Accomplishments

You will be measured on the goals that you accomplish, but nobody will have as much incentive as you yourself for keeping track of exactly what you have done. Keep a separate notebook, planner, or digital file to list the work that you do even as often as each week, and then highlight the big accomplishments more clearly. When it comes time to discuss your work with your superiors in either informal discussions or the year-end review, you will have documentation on what happened. Nobody remembers everything from a whole year's worth of work. Don't miss out on credit simply because too many accomplishments were left by the wayside.

> **TIP**
>
> Professionals are always negotiating within and across jobs. Make your next negotiation easier by actively cultivating your network of colleagues and your assignments, and by making sure your superiors know of your hard work.

SITUATION 4: WITHDRAWN OFFERS

What if they rescind the offer?

While offers are only *very* rarely withdrawn during the negotiation itself (and in those cases, it is usually due to egregious behavior such as lying or extreme demands), offers are unfortunately more commonly withdrawn after the deal is done (but for other reasons). Typically, this happens either because an employing company is experiencing economic hardship and thus has eliminated your future job, or because the company has just been merged or reorganized in some fashion with another company. Merger or reorganization may create lots of duplicity in roles, and thus jobs are sometimes eliminated for that reason. In both of these situations, there are typically internal layoffs occurring as well. In fact, if you have heard the words "layoff" or "buyout" during your interviews, you might want to look elsewhere. If you had a contract that is terminated before you even start, walking away is probably your best option. But you could also pursue seeking either some sort of "separation" compensation and/or legal action, if you are so inclined.

You could first try to speak with your would-be employers, remind them that they have placed you in a difficult situation, and ask what options are available. You may wish to ask about (1) the possibility of a separation package of some sort, (2) the possibility of being given preference for other opportunities available within the organization, and (3) the possibility of having the company's HR department aid your search. As we alluded to earlier, if the organization is experiencing economic hardship or is being bought out, then the possibility of any of this is unlikely. Also, be aware that emotions will run high from both parties.

The last option available is to consider legal avenues. People rarely benefit from a legal battle of this kind, but you could consult an attorney to find out where you stand. Remember to ask: How long do you anticipate the legal interaction to last, and what do you estimate the costs will run? Although this is undeterminable, you may wish to ask for a best guess. Keep in mind that a sizable portion of legal costs are incurred *after* a legal decision is rendered, such as in the appeals process, so you may wish to assess all the possible options (and their resulting costs) that could potentially occur once the dispute is settled in court. Weigh the costs on your time as well before you embark on this path.

> **TIP**
>
> Our frank and simple advice for when an employer withdraws an offer is to cut your losses and move on to another organization.

SITUATION 5: THE CHANGING DEAL

What do I do if my employer is not living up to the employment terms?

This situation is more common than having an offer withdrawn. Typically this situation arises because of an unintentional oversight as opposed to a deliberate choice of action by the employer. In fact, whether or not the "oversight" was intentional, it is probably in your best interest to assume that your employer had the best intentions, and proceed accordingly.

Here is a quiz to illustrate this: You have been employed to manage the manufacturing portion of a large auto glass manufacturer, close to the school where you are continuing your studies in supply chain management. After working for a year, you have heard the rumor that this company will no longer reimburse tuition for educational expenses. Which of the following options do you feel best describes how you should react?

   A. You immediately go to your boss (the plant manager), to ask her about this rumor. You remind her that she had committed to paying for your classes, and tell her that you are submitting your tuition for reimbursement and that you will expect them to pay it per the terms of your employment contract.

B. You bring up the topic the next time you are having a conversation anyway by mentioning that your coursework is making you a better employee. You hope she will bring up the topic of tuition reimbursement herself, but if she does not, you will let her know that you are concerned about some rumors you heard and tell her that you really need her help to make this happen.

C. You ignore the rumor and submit your bill when the time comes. If they do not pay, you intend to consult an attorney.

Your intuitive choice here may indicate how willing you are to take on a confrontational approach in a negotiation, and while each option has some merit, getting both sides to work on the problem together generally nets the best outcomes. Remember that relationships pave the way to solutions, and this situation is a good example of how using a joint problem-solving approach (one like option B) is likely to get you the best result.

The problem with being overly direct and confrontational (as in option A) is that it implies both threat and blame. Both have a tendency to cause a defensive stance in the other side, which can lead people to further entrench into their position or even to hold a grudge they may later act upon. Instead, you want your employer to move in a direction that is compatible with your interests. A direct but more relationship-based approach suggests the consideration of your interests, without a sense of blame. Furthermore, this option gives you the best shot at avoiding a sense of disrespect and hopefully preserving the relationship. The third option might avoid confrontation initially, but includes a bomb (the legal course of action). If you were to proceed to legal action without first discussing the issue with your manager, it would most likely damage your working relationship beyond repair.

Now let's make the situation even more complicated. Let's say you approach your boss, and her response is to tell you that she never promised you tuition reimbursement, and now that the company does not support the decision any longer, she will no longer cover this expense. Now you have moved from a sticky situation into a dispute—defined as a rejected claim in which two parties disagree about what are the facts and/or the appropriate course of action going forward. When you find yourself in a dispute, there are generally four different avenues of argument you can present to the other side when you get the chance to discuss it.[2] While each has advantages and drawbacks, one in particular (discussing your interests, #4 below) has the best chance for peaceably resolving disputes. Let's look at each in turn.

1. *Information Exchange:* You can go over the facts and events and potentially fall prey to an "I said versus you said" type of conversation where you find that you do not see eye to eye on the basics. This, in fact, is probably why you found yourself in a dispute in the first place. That being said, there can be some merit to letting both sides vent about their impressions of what happened to clear the air on the story that each is holding onto, and then try to move forward next.

2. *Rights:* You can discuss, with each other and potentially with legal counsel, who is in the right and who is in the wrong in a legal sense. What exactly does the contract state? If you were to go to court on this matter, who would most likely prevail? The problem with these kinds of arguments is twofold. First, legal opinions are often just that—opinions—and it is not uncommon for both sides to be told by their respective lawyers that they are the ones who have the stronger case. Unfortunately, despite careful wording, the language used in contracts of all sorts often leaves some unanticipated wiggle room after the fact. Second, statements to the other side describing the legal aspects of your case are almost always taken as threats, and tend to inspire the other side to escalate the situation until you may indeed find yourself in court when it does not serve your best interests.

3. *Power:* Often related to rights, this has to do with what you can make the other do simply because it is your wish, not necessarily because of what is in your contract. For example, let's say in the scenario above that you, the employee, are the only one with some specific expertise and the manager is desperate to keep you happy. Then, whether or not it is in your contract, your manager may try to do all she can to find the money to reimburse your classes. On the other hand, if your manager has been told to reduce her headcount anyway, your problem could be all she needs to decide that you should be terminated, in no small part because you may be entitled to this extra perk. But discussing these kinds of threats can again make you feel like adversaries, and may make you more likely to end up walking away from each other than solving the dispute in a reasonable way.

4. *Interests:* Last and most influential is the use of interest-based arguments. By this we mean explaining to your boss why you are making your request, and what will happen afterward. Similarly, if you

can ask questions to understand why your boss is presenting a particular decision, you might be able to look for alternative solutions together. For example, if in the tuition-reimbursement case you explained, "I want you to understand where I'm coming from. The courses I'm taking have given me lots of insights into how to do this job more effectively, and the rest of the program promises to be just as valuable. If tuition reimbursement is cut entirely, I will have to withdraw from the program. You have invested a lot of money already and I have made tremendous personal sacrifice carving time out of my evenings to take these classes. Completing them is very important to me and will also provide greater benefits for the company. I understand that the budget is tight—what if I take one class at a time instead of two? We would cut the strain on the budget in half but I would be able to continue making progress in this important area."

The rule of thumb in these situations is that it is easier to move from an interests-based discussion to exchanging threats based on rights or power if you need to, but it is much more difficult to de-escalate the conversation back from rights and power to being interest-based. If you have the chance to initiate the conversation, interests are where you want to start and stay. Even if you hear the other side offering up comments based on rights and power, though, you still have the opportunity to try to steer the conversation back to more productive ground by gently suggesting a retreat (to interest-based alternatives), such as "We have both looked over the contract and we can spend our time going back and forth about what we are entitled to, but perhaps we could see if there is a solution that would meet both of our needs without using lawyers."

> **TIP**
>
> If you find that your employers are no longer living up to their end of the deal, stay calm and focus on solving the problem while preserving the relationship. There is always time to get ugly later.

SUMMARY

After finishing a successful job negotiation, you should of course take some time to celebrate; but unfortunately, the work for a savvy job negotiator is not over. The next step of the job negotiation process—setting the stage for the next round of negotiations—begins almost immediately. This next round may be internal with your current company or perhaps with an entirely new company. By setting the stage now for the next job negotiation, you will make the future negotiations easier, and you may even open up new and different opportunities. Take the time to prepare for a successful next job negotiation by taking responsibility for managing your professional relationships, carving out the work you want to be doing, and keeping track of everything that you have accomplished. If you find yourself facing the darker side of a job negotiation process (like a contract being withdrawn or an employer not living up to the deal), seek to discover if there are friendly ways out of the situation and, if not, consider walking away. When things do not go according to plan, remain focused on what you and the other side want to see out of a final agreement, and resort to legal or power struggles only as a last resort. Again, you should feel good about seeing your job negotiation through to completion. But don't rest on your laurels too long—get to work preparing for the next job-related negotiation.

NOTES

1. Granovetter, M. S., The strength of weak ties. *American Journal of Sociology*, 78, 1973: 1360–1380.

2. Ury, W., J. M. Brett, and S. B. Goldberg, *Getting disputes resolved: Designing systems to cut the costs of conflict*. San Francisco, CA: Jossey-Bass, 1988.

TEN

The Top 10 Most Important Things to Remember

Job negotiations are both important and intimidating. We hope that by reading this book, you have become more comfortable and confident about the ins and outs of the process. In this last chapter, we summarize the top 10 key points from the entire book. Each time you approach a new job negotiation opportunity, you can easily review these 10 critical insights before you begin negotiating. They are presented in a format of "Traps then Tips."

TRAP 1: NOT NEGOTIATING

TIPS

Remain positive about the possibility of getting a better employment package than the one you were initially offered. Just remember that the overarching theme to successful job negotiations is to be respectful and reasonable at all times. Be sure to keep this guiding principle before you, and then jump in. There is some truth to the adage that you get half of what you ask for, and none of what you don't.

TRAP 2: NOT PREPARING EFFECTIVELY FOR THE JOB NEGOTIATION

TIPS

Preparation may be tedious, but it is the single best tool in your arsenal. Many people think they can "wing it" effectively, but for the most part they are wrong. It is worth your time to prepare well. Preparation involves knowing your minimum needs and your alternatives to the negotiation (another offer in the wings, staying put at your current job, unemployment, etc.). In addition, you should do your homework and know a lot about the company, their business, and their style of negotiating (in part by talking to as many insiders as you can both before and during the interview process). Become absolutely perfect with your delivery of key points by practicing your well-crafted "stories" and answers to tough questions ahead of time. Prepare good questions to ask them to demonstrate your engagement with *this* job. Know the issues to negotiate and truly understand the value to you of each and every element in the job negotiation and what you are willing to trade or compromise on to get the items that are more valuable. Finally, preparing means not only knowing yourself and your situation, but also thinking through what the company is likely to say and do based on your estimates of where they might be coming from.

TRAP 3: TALKING ABOUT NUMBERS (THAT IS, NEGOTIATING) TOO SOON IN THE PROCESS

TIPS

You do not want to start negotiating before it is time to do so. If at all possible, we highly advise letting your future employer put the first packaged offer on the table. If you start with numbers yourself, even by reporting a desired salary range, you run the risk of either under- or overestimating your worth to them. Either can be damaging to your final bottom line. In addition, you ideally want to see their offer *in writing* before you get to the nitty-gritty aspects of the deal (but certainly before you agree to it). Most of the time, waiting for a written offer before negotiating is just a formality. Occasionally, doing so will avoid a sticky situation in which the final deal does not accurately represent what was promised to you verbally. In short, don't jump the gun by either putting your own numbers on the table first or by getting too far in the process without written confirmation of the details.

TRAP 4: PAYING TOO MUCH ATTENTION TO THE BASE SALARY NUMBER AT THE EXPENSE OF OTHER ISSUES

TIPS

You need to keep all of the issues in your mind, and put as many as possible into the discussion. Establish your priorities by considering the overall value of the deal to you, not just the base salary. Focus on a good balance between the long-term gains (career building, relationships, and/or family needs) and short-term gains (salary, bonuses).

TRAP 5: NOT EXPLAINING WHY YOU WANT WHAT YOU ARE REQUESTING, AND NOT FRAMING IT TO SEEM FAIR

TIPS

Remember that you will want to provide a rational justification for every one of your requests. Not only does it make you seem more reasonable, but it may help the hiring manager justify the concession to others inside the firm, or finding another way to meet the underlying interests. Remember the three widely accepted routes to explaining fairness: (1) it is fair to want what others like you are getting; (2) it is fair to want compensation for your particular contributions or skills; and (3) it is fair to want help for reasonable needs such as student loans or moving expenses.

TRAP 6: ASKING FOR TOO MUCH "JUST TO SEE"

TIPS

Remember that the company you are dealing with is looking at you as a potential colleague in addition to negotiating your contract, so pay attention to the impression that you are making. The "respectful and reasonable" rule should underlie the entire relationship. The relationship starts the minute you initiate contact, and continues through the give-and-take phase of the negotiation.

TRAP 7: MISSING DETAILS BY NOT LISTENING CAREFULLY OR BY GETTING OVERWHELMED

TIPS

Make sure you place your full attention on everything the other side is saying, and are not thinking ahead to the next question you want to ask. Take a break from the negotiation any time you feel emotions getting the better of you, or feel your attention waning for any other reason. You are not typically required to complete the job negotiation in one sitting.

TRAP 8: SENDING UNCLEAR SIGNALS

TIPS

Remember that you are in sales from the moment you send your resume until the day you start the job. Part of what you need to sell is your enthusiasm for the job and the company. Don't fall into the all-too-common trap of letting your negotiating nerves come across as indifference about the job. Be especially sure to watch the cues you send via e-mail, as tone and intent are even more easily misunderstood in this medium. In fact, though e-mail can be useful for simple questions, anything more than routine should, if possible, be discussed face to face.

TRAP 9: GIVING TOO MUCH INFORMATION TO A HEADHUNTER OR OTHER INTERMEDIARY

TIPS

Two general strategies will help you use a headhunter most effectively: (1) as much as possible, proceed offer by offer without giving absolutes about where your actual cutoff values are (that is, the minimum you would take); and (2) maintain a direct line of communication with the hiring manager even when going through a headhunter. This way, there is a "backup" channel of communication in case things do not proceed smoothly through the headhunter.

TRAP 10: LYING OR MISREPRESENTING YOURSELF IN ANY WAY

TIPS

This strategy *could* work for you, but it could also backfire and have some pretty unpleasant consequences. But even if it works, we urge you to think about whether this is the way you want to get ahead.

The bottom line is that if you are a business professional changing your employment terms in any way, you might as well strive for the best terms. Read this book, keep these points in mind, and the process will unfold in a more systematic and less anxiety-provoking manner.

Finally, please feel free to drop us a note with your own stories and experiences. We would love to hear how this book influenced your job negotiation, and may even use your story (anonymously) in future editions of this book.

We can be reached at feedback@jobnegotiationessentials.com.

Good luck and happy negotiating!

Appendix A

Planning Table: The Seven Key Insights for Effective Planning

You	The Firm
1a. What do you *need* out of this offer (i.e., what are the deal-breakers for you?)	**1b.** What do you think the company *need* out of a candidate?
1.	1.
2.	2.
3.	3.
4.	4.
5.	5.
2a. What do you *want* out of this offer (i.e., what's your target/ideal job look like)?	**2b.** What do you think the company *want* out of a candidate?
1.	1.
2.	2.
3.	3.
4.	4.
5.	5.

(Continued)

(Continued)

You	The Firm

3. What would a really great offer look like for you, roughly? (A realistic stretch, not a "pie in the sky.")

4. What would a minimally acceptable offer look like for you, roughly?

5. What information should you make sure you share with the other side to explain to them how you will meet their *needs* well and even fulfill some of their *wants*?

6a. What options do you have other than this job?

6b. What options do you think the company has other than you?

7. Based on the above, how powerful do you think you are relative to the other side (i.e., how badly do you think they need you, and how badly do you want this job)?

Appendix B

Potential Issues

Note that even this is not an exhaustive list, but rather a sample of possible issues. You will find that different professions will have different issues to consider. In addition, not all of these items are things that will be (or even should be) negotiable.

Salary
- Base salary (annual compensation)

Bonuses and Other Monetary Benefits
- Annual bonus (performance-based)
  - Mid-year prorated or fixed-amount bonus for first year if applicable
  - Automatic versus performance-based salary increases
- Signing bonus
- Stock options/equity
- Profit sharing
- Tuition (or training) reimbursement/conference travel
- Commissions

Timing Issues
- Start date
- Vacation time (specific time of year)

- Vacation length
  - Unused days carry over to next year?
  - Payment for unused days?
- Annual performance review/salary review
- Time for professional training/classes/conferences
- Maternity/paternity leave

Professional Relationships and Support

- Immediate supervisor
- Administrative support
- Performance reviews

Relocation Issues

- Moving costs
- Expenses during transition
- Hotel expenses
- Temporary housing
- Home selling assistance (selling your current home)
- Home buying assistance (your new residence)

Insurance

- Coverage start date
- Spousal/family coverage (Does employer pay premium?)

Miscellaneous

- Technology/accessories (laptop, PDA, etc.)
- Technology upgrade schedule (e.g., new equipment after two years)
- Travel expenses (car and meal reimbursements, etc.)
- Retirement plan

Appendix C

Online Salary Information

Keep in mind that the best source (i.e., more specific to your career) of salary information is from (1) your personal network, (2) the career center of the school you graduated from, or (3) industry-specific associations. These websites provide general benchmarks and should not be used as concrete evidence for your market worth to the firm, but instead should just give you a place to start. HR representatives will need better justification for your salary requests than "I saw on some website that I should be making X."

http://www.salaryexpert.com
http://www.salary.com
http://www.payscale.com
http://www.glassdoor.com
http://www.homefair.com
http://jobstar.org

Index

About the Authors

Terri R. Kurtzberg, PhD, is associate professor of management and global business at the Rutgers Business School–Newark and New Brunswick at Rutgers University, New Jersey, where she teaches negotiations and organizational behavior. She received her PhD from the Kellogg Graduate School of Management at Northwestern University, Evanston, Illinois. Dr. Kurtzberg has recently been honored with two teaching awards and one research award. Her articles on negotiations and electronic communications have been cited by *Fortune* magazine, the *New York Times*, CNN.com, BBC World Service Radio, and CBS Radio. Her work has been published in journals such as *Journal of Applied Psychology, Organizational Behavior and Human Decision Processes, International Journal of Conflict Management*, and *Group Dynamics: Theory, Practice, and Research.*

Charles E. Naquin, PhD, is associate professor of management at DePaul's Kellstadt Graduate School of Business, where he teaches negotiations and organizational behavior. He received his PhD from the Kellogg Graduate School of Management at Northwestern University, Evanston, Illinois. Dr. Naquin's undergraduate work was completed at the University of Texas at Austin. His articles on negotiations and decision making have been published in journals such as the *Journal of Applied Psychology* and *Organizational Behavior and Human Decision Processes*, and his work has been cited by *Fortune* magazine, the *New York Times*, CNN.com, BBC World Service Radio, and CBS Radio.